THE CODER'S PATH TO WEALTH AND INDEPENDENCE

Mark Beckner

Apress®

The Coder's Path to Wealth and Independence

Copyright © 2014 by Mark Beckner

This work is subject to copyright. All rights are reserved by the Publisher, whether the whole or part of the material is concerned, specifically the rights of translation, reprinting, reuse of illustrations, recitation, broadcasting, reproduction on microfilms or in any other physical way, and transmission or information storage and retrieval, electronic adaptation, computer software, or by similar or dissimilar methodology now known or hereafter developed. Exempted from this legal reservation are brief excerpts in connection with reviews or scholarly analysis or material supplied specifically for the purpose of being entered and executed on a computer system, for exclusive use by the purchaser of the work. Duplication of this publication or parts thereof is permitted only under the provisions of the Copyright Law of the Publisher's location, in its current version, and permission for use must always be obtained from Springer. Permissions for use may be obtained through RightsLink at the Copyright Clearance Center. Violations are liable to prosecution under the respective Copyright Law.

ISBN-13 (pbk): 978-1-4842-0422-1

ISBN-13 (electronic): 978-1-4842-0421-4

Trademarked names, logos, and images may appear in this book. Rather than use a trademark symbol with every occurrence of a trademarked name, logo, or image we use the names, logos, and images only in an editorial fashion and to the benefit of the trademark owner, with no intention of infringement of the trademark.

The use in this publication of trade names, trademarks, service marks, and similar terms, even if they are not identified as such, is not to be taken as an expression of opinion as to whether or not they are subject to proprietary rights.

While the advice and information in this book are believed to be true and accurate at the date of publication, neither the authors nor the editors nor the publisher can accept any legal responsibility for any errors or omissions that may be made. The publisher makes no warranty, express or implied, with respect to the material contained herein.

Managing Director: Welmoed Spahr
Acquisitions Editor: Jeff Olson
Editorial Board: Steve Anglin, Gary Cornell, Louise Corrigan, James DeWolf, Jonathan Gennick, Robert Hutchinson, Michelle Lowman, James Markham, Matthew Moodie, Jeff Olson, Jeffrey Pepper, Douglas Pundick, Ben Renow-Clarke, Gwenan Spearing, Steve Weiss
Coordinating Editor: Rita Fernando
Copy Editor: William McManus, Catherine O'Hala
Compositor: SPi Global
Indexer: SPi Global
Cover Designer: Anna Ishchenko

Distributed to the book trade worldwide by Springer Science+Business Media New York, 233 Spring Street, 6th Floor, New York, NY 10013. Phone 1-800-SPRINGER, fax (201) 348-4505, e-mail orders-ny@springer-sbm.com, or visit www.springeronline.com. Apress Media, LLC is a California LLC and the sole member (owner) is Springer Science + Business Media Finance Inc (SSBM Finance Inc). SSBM Finance Inc is a Delaware corporation.

For information on translations, please e-mail rights@apress.com, or visit www.apress.com.

Apress and friends of ED books may be purchased in bulk for academic, corporate, or promotional use. eBook versions and licenses are also available for most titles. For more information, reference our Special Bulk Sales–eBook Licensing web page at www.apress.com/bulk-sales.

Any source code or other supplementary materials referenced by the author in this text is available to readers at www.apress.com. For detailed information about how to locate your book's source code, go to www.apress.com/source-code/.

Apress Business: The Unbiased Source of Business Information

Apress business books provide essential information and practical advice, each written for practitioners by recognized experts. Busy managers and professionals in all areas of the business world—and at all levels of technical sophistication—look to our books for the actionable ideas and tools they need to solve problems, update and enhance their professional skills, make their work lives easier, and capitalize on opportunity.

Whatever the topic on the business spectrum—entrepreneurship, finance, sales, marketing, management, regulation, information technology, among others—Apress has been praised for providing the objective information and unbiased advice you need to excel in your daily work life. Our authors have no axes to grind; they understand they have one job only—to deliver up-to-date, accurate information simply, concisely, and with deep insight that addresses the real needs of our readers.

It is increasingly hard to find information—whether in the news media, on the Internet, and now all too often in books—that is even-handed and has your best interests at heart. We therefore hope that you enjoy this book, which has been carefully crafted to meet our standards of quality and unbiased coverage.

We are always interested in your feedback or ideas for new titles. Perhaps you'd even like to write a book yourself. Whatever the case, reach out to us at editorial@apress.com and an editor will respond swiftly. Incidentally, at the back of this book, you will find a list of useful related titles. Please visit us at www.apress.com to sign up for newsletters and discounts on future purchases.

The Apress Business Team

To Ciro Augustine and Iyer Blue, may you both have an abundance of freedom and joy in your lives, and to your mother who keeps us healthy in spirit, mind, and body.

Contents

Contents

Foreword

I am one of you, a coder. I prefer listening over speaking, reading over partying; I love to create but dislike self-promotion; and I favor working on my own over brainstorming in groups. I am one of you, a highly skilled coder, a developer, a software architect, a product designer—and I was, for over two decades, developing "cool" products that I did not believe in. To me, the focus of life and achievement in the corporate world was defined by review cycles and competition in the rewards curve rather than customer satisfaction.

Sure, we coders are paid well, well above population averages, and with that money we pay off mortgages and car loans to trade them in for bigger ones. Every once in a while we take off on a week-long vacation, only to return to excessive work hours to compensate for the time off. The happiness such experiences bring us is very event related and transient. Yet somehow, the wealth and independence we crave escape us.

Not anymore!

I have not met Mark Beckner in person. However, I have been profoundly impacted by the many phone and e-mail conversations we have had. While his technical and marketing skills are well known and chronicled by publications, his mentoring abilities are less well known. He is a great teacher, always using practical examples that I could relate to. Through our conversations, he talked me out of my routine and into the brave new world of launching a successful and ethical business that has led to independence and wealth—wealth not just measured in dollars but in realizing the goals and aspirations I have in this life.

A few weeks ago, Mark mentioned this book to me, and I was excited that he found a way to scale his outreach to many more coders like me. As a beta reader of this extraordinary book, I can tell you that it has the power to permanently change your life, filling it with wealth and, more importantly, independence.

Mark shares in this book many gripping, real-life incidents to make his points. It takes you through the mechanics of a business—structure, ethics, marketing, sales, contracts, and even travel—along with the more spiritual dimensions of running a successful independent business: the philosophical, personal, and social aspects of creating new business along with such varied topics as health, personal vitality, social obligations, and charity.

This book is topical from a technology standpoint because so many substantive changes are occurring in the computer software and services industries. We have not only the advent of the cloud and its massive compute power on a global scale, but also the Internet of Things (IoT) and the immense amount of data generated—and all this rendered via hand-held and mobile devices. Essentially there is something "new" that will enable every category of coder to succeed. To deal with the onslaught of new technologies, enterprises around the world will have to hire fresh talent. What an opportunity to transform yourself from a skilled programmer stuck in employment into a highly creative and effective businessperson leveraging the skills you already have. The lessons in this book provide a framework to help plan and execute this transformation.

I would be remiss if I did not mention a few of my favorite sections from Chapter 12—a chapter I especially connected with. First, the introduction describing an abundance mentality stood out to me. Give and it shall be given unto you. Mark writes, "Your greatest tool in continuously growing your business and increasing your own personal wealth is to use your finances liberally. Someone who is generous, and who is constantly looking for ways to use the resources that come their way for the betterment of not only themselves but the world around them, is someone who will see constant opportunity and great levels of wealth, freedom, and success."

Second, the "Competition" section of Chapter 12 resonated with me. Mark writes, "You are not a competitor and you do not have competition. There may be others who are in the same business as you, and who could potentially take clients from you, but you should not view them as competition. Instead, view them as potential partners or collaborators. Anyone who is in the same business as you has the ability to help you grow, and you have the ability to help them grow. Any work you do together has the potential to create new opportunities, building something where nothing was before."

Given the broad coverage of this book, I am sure you will find your own points of connection that resonate deeply.

This book is about me. Its ideas set me on my path and gave me the courage to take a new direction with my own business, Maarg Labs. After reading this book, you, too, will set forth on your own path to wealth and independence.

I take great pleasure in writing this foreword and recommending this book.

Namaste!

Suren K. Machiraju
Founder, Maarg Labs
www.maarglabs.com
November 1, 2014

About the Author

Mark Beckner is a technical consultant specializing in business strategy and enterprise application integration. He runs his own consulting firm, Inotek Consulting Group, LLC, delivering innovative solutions to large corporations and small businesses. His projects have included engagements with numerous clients throughout the United States and South America, and range in nature from mobile application development to complete integration solutions. He advises and assists developers and consultants in launching their own independent, successful, and fulfilling careers. He has authored a variety of technical books, including *BizTalk 2013 EDI for Health Care*, *BizTalk 2013 Recipes*, and *Microsoft Dynamics CRM API Development*, and has spoken at a number of venues, including Microsoft TechEd. Beckner, his wife Sara, and his boys Ciro and Iyer live somewhere in the rugged deserts and/or mountains of the American West. His web site is www.inotekgroup.com, and he can be contacted directly at mbeckner@inotekgroup.com.

Acknowledgments

In any career, there are countless people who open doors of opportunity. How much of us is truly ourselves and how much is a synthesis of people and ideas we've been influenced by is something we can never know. One thing is for certain: whatever independence we have is based on our interactions with those we've come into contact with and those who have come before us, and any wealth that we have is due to a system that allows for generosity and creation and the people who support this system. None of us is separate from the whole.

Introduction

This book is for coders who want to take control of their personal and professional lives.

Jean-Jacques Rousseau, in *The Social Contract*, wrote, "Man was born free, but everywhere he is in chains. This man believes that he is the master of others, and still he is more of a slave than they are." The reason that most people are in chains is that they do not know the path to freedom. My purpose in this book is to show you the path to freedom through the use of your technical skills.

This path harnesses the inherent power of business to enable you to reach personal and professional independence and wealth. With this wealth and independence, you will have the freedom to pursue any activity, attain any goal, and realize any dream that you choose.

I cover many topics, always emphasizing that your ability to succeed in the pursuit of wealth and independence is contingent on your whole state of being, professional and personal. Your thinking, your discipline, your dedication, your health, and your use of resources play a direct and significant role in the success of your business, and will determine whether or not you will be able to achieve the goals that you set for yourself.

While there may be many paths that can lead to financial prosperity, I guarantee that if you approach your work as outlined in this book, you will not only be able to make significantly more money than most others in the technical field, you will also be able to achieve great things in your personal life and will be an asset to the world. You will have abundance, and will be able to give abundantly.

You are in a position to control your life. The technical industry affords freedoms unlike any other trade, and it is completely up to you whether you pursue these freedoms or let them pass you by. You don't have to be a slave of any system, or at the command of any boss. You no longer have to work in a cubicle, commute by plane, live apart from your family, or sacrifice your health for an unrealistic project timeline.

In short, this book will show you how to be the master of yourself, slave to no one. Pursue wealth and independence and live to your highest potential.

—Mark Beckner
October 29, 2014

Roadmap to Content

Chapter 1, "Travel: The Power of Staying in Motion"

There is value and purpose in being able to work from anywhere and to be in continuous motion. The notion of movement in this regard is powerful and encompasses both physical and mental movement. As you progress through the various stages of business, the nature of this movement will change, and you will be able to meet it on your terms and leverage it to create the outcomes you require. This chapter outlines techniques for making business travel satisfying, travel that leads to opportunity and that supports your ambitions for success and independence.

Chapter 2, "Skills: Foundations in Programming and Business"

Programming is inherently creative, and it can be leveraged along with related skills to create a highly successful practice. Embracing the true nature of business will create value, lead to opportunities, and open paths to a greater and more rewarding life. This chapter describes how to develop and apply programming, architecture, strategy, and other skills to create a business that succeeds.

Chapter 3, "Discipline and Education: The Importance of Continuous Improvement"

The discipline behind a successful practice includes a commitment to order, professionalism, communication, availability, and personal growth. Success comes through a combination of strong personal discipline and constant education. This chapter explores techniques and approaches to ensure continuous improvement of your business and yourself.

Chapter 4, "Ethics: The Foundation of Relationships and Business"

Developing and maintaining core ethical values will lay a foundation for strong business relationships. Failure to conduct business ethically puts your business and those you work with at risk and limits your ability to succeed. This chapter covers the ethical use of skills, ethical communication and billing practices, and ethics in professional relationships.

Chapter 5, "Structuring Your Business: Taxes, Insurance, and Protecting Yourself"

Business structures are critical, professionalism is a requirement, and insurance is a necessity. This chapter outlines options for starting and structuring your business, describes what types of insurance you need, and explains how to create a level of separation between your professional and private assets.

Chapter 6, "Advertising and Marketing: The Science of Lead Creation"

Taking specific actions in advertising and marketing will produce results. This chapter covers how to advertise, how to market, how to acquire clients and project work, and how to apply these activities to open the path to continued business opportunities.

Chapter 7, "Sales: The Art of Networking, Prospecting, and Closing"

Advertising and marketing are the science of client acquisition, while prospecting and sales are the art. Rainmakers, those who are able to bring in business even when times are hard, have certain skills and methods that you will learn in this chapter and enable you to prosper.

Chapter 8, "Proposals and Contracts: Trust, Simplicity, and Getting Paid"

Focusing relentlessly on strong communication with clients will ensure that you have a clear path to creating proposals and contracts that are accepted every time. This chapter offers techniques to come to agreement efficiently on scope, level of effort, and deliverables to ensure that you minimize the time it takes to start your engagements and maximize your success.

Chapter 9, "Fees and Income: Creating a High-Dollar Revenue Stream"

A variety of pricing structures and models will allow you to create high-value engagements for yourself and for your clients. You have immense flexibility in how you engage, and your approach to fees and pricing should reflect that. This chapters explains how to utilize and combine hourly, fixed fee, and retainer models to create multiple powerful revenue streams.

Chapter 10, "Goal Setting: The Engine Behind Your Success"

Those who set goals on a daily, weekly, and annual basis move ahead faster than those who do not. When you put your mind to it, you can get more done in less time than ever before. Setting goals—and accomplishing them— is a powerful means to create forward momentum in both your personal and professional life. This chapter provides techniques for identifying your goals and seeing them come to fruition.

Chapter 11, "Growth and Expansion: Handling Success"

Success will come—but you must continually change in order to support the inevitable growth and demand. This chapter covers how to sustain multiple projects, when to include subcontractors, the case for hiring employees, and how to retain your independence and freedom in the face of success.

Chapter 12, "Business Investing and Wealth Utilization: The Abundance Mentality"

Making money is good. But money is like energy—once created, it must flow in order to allow more to be created. The wealth you generate should be used to improve your business, create opportunities for others, support good works, and ultimately be put back into the system. This chapter covers ways to approach money, uses of income, paths to increased income, and other related topics.

Chapter 13, "Health: Personal Vitality and the Impact on Your Business"

Movement must occur at all levels of life—mental, spiritual, and physical. Business is in support of life, and life must, in turn, be in support of business for maximum success. This chapter outlines tangible steps you can take to support your health, and describes the positive impact that healthy living can have on your business.

Chapter 14, "Freedom Through Business: Wealth, Dreams, and Independence"

The truly successful entrepreneur has not only financial abundance, but great freedom in both business and in private life. The ability to pursue the activities that interest you, attain personal dreams, and invest time in private pursuits are all measures of wealth and success. As this chapter explains, through an intelligent application of the various topics outlined in previous chapters, you will be able to attain true wealth and freedom through programming and business.

Travel

The Power of Staying in Motion

An object at rest stays at rest, and an object in motion stays in motion with the same speed and in the same direction unless acted upon by an unbalanced force.

—Sir Isaac Newton's First Law of Motion

The coder's path to prosperity and independence is paved through continual movement; there is nothing more critical to your success. As Newton's First Law states, an object at rest stays at rest. Therefore, to overcome the inertia and stagnation that can show up easily in any career, you must put yourself in motion; be part of the power that fuels your personal and professional growth, and embrace the opportunities that present themselves to you.

This book opens with a chapter on business travel, because motion is at the core of your ability to prosper and grow professionally. Your work begins by moving from a typical coder's stationary existence to a mobile, professional lifestyle. After you've determined how to become mobile, you must understand the difference between nonessential travel and travel critical to the success of your business. Mastering the art of business travel takes time and constant review, and it is best complemented with a pattern of thought that is also fluid and mobile. You should be open to opportunity, view everything as transitory, and look constantly at how to alter your environment to better your situation.

Your goal should be to push yourself into profitable and meaningful motion— while avoiding unnecessary and wasteful travel—and let the momentum carry you to the highest levels of success.

Rule Business travel is critical to your ability to achieve a high level of success. It is essential to your growth and prosperity. It is also the very thing that can limit the flow of opportunity, drain your time and vitality, and ultimately create an unfulfilling, marginally lucrative, and highly dependent professional life. You must balance the necessity for business travel with the underlying need to grow your business and your options.

From Rest to Motion

As a coder, you very likely come from a background that is not dependent on travel. Coding generally starts as an autonomous occupation—developers are hired into companies that provide them a cubicle and expect them to move as infrequently as possible. Those of us who are attracted to this job are often introverted. However, although the reality of coding in a nonprofessional environment may be that it is a solitary endeavor, in the professional world— especially in later stages of a career path—the work environment is made up of constant interaction, meetings, dialogues, and social activities.

CASE STUDY

In college, when I decided to focus on computer science, one of the deciding factors was that I wanted a career in which I could work alone, with limited social interaction. My understanding of the programmer's environment was wrong. Computer science is a highly interactive and social environment, especially for those who wish to become prosperous in the field.

Going from a stationary resting position to a mobile position takes some effort, but it is an essential step to moving toward independence. You must harness the power of travel to aid you in your growth and success. There are several ways to get yourself in motion. Consider the following:

1. **Reach out to your contacts**. You've worked with companies and individuals in the past and, assuming you haven't burned all of your bridges, you have many potential opportunities available. Reach out to these contacts. Let them know where you are in your career and what type of work you are looking for. Tell them how you can help them; make them aware of your evolving skill set and availability. Letting people know you are alive, that you are available, that you have current in-demand skills, and that you are looking for opportunities is the quickest way to making things happen.

2. **Take a trip.** This strategy might be new to you, but it could help generate new business leads. Visit your contacts—past clients and employers—periodically. Offer to take them to lunch. Few people will turn you down. Use that time to catch up and indicate your willingness to take on new work. These networks are important to maintain. Spending money without any immediate payback may be new to you, but it may help you reap rewards later. This strategy puts you into the energetic flow of where you want to be, and it will open doors that wouldn't open under other circumstances. Sometimes you simply have to pack your bags and hit the road to make things happen.

3. **Take on contract work.** For those of you who have no contacts and are just getting started in your career, consider engaging in contract work at a remote location. There are thousands of temporary onsite jobs in the information technology (IT) world, with companies looking for individuals with a specific skill set to augment their teams—and this type of work is fairly easy to find. Although remote contract work is career suicide after you have established your successful business, it is an option for getting yourself in motion early in your career.

4. **Work with a consulting firm.** A short stint with a consulting firm can also have a great impact on your career, your contacts, and your momentum. Most firms require their personnel to travel for work. Most likely, you will have an opportunity to work with platforms and applications to which you may not otherwise be exposed, which will enhance your skill set. In addition, the people you meet and with whom you work will become invaluable contacts, if cultivated correctly. Many of these contacts will go on to greater things in their own career, which could provide you with better opportunities. This strategy, like contract work, is for the junior programmer, and likely isn't something you would do beyond the earliest stages of your career.

The Two Types of Business Travel

There are two types of business travel. The first is *critical business travel*, which allows for high-impact programming, project advancement, relationship building, and sales. Critical business travel is enriching and rewarding, highly valuable to you and your client, and easy to sustain. It is a recurring, positive requirement for the health of your business.

The second type is *noncritical business travel*—an often necessary but bitter aspect of early careers, and a staple of experienced professionals. Noncritical business travel can be wasteful, inefficient, limiting, and invasive. and should be viewed as a toxin that needs to be removed from your environment as quickly as possible if you wish to prosper and attain new levels of professional growth.

■ **Rule** Business travel includes both long-distance and local client visits. For example, I know people in metropolitan areas that spend hours every day traveling from one client site to the next. In a day or two, they put in more travel time than someone traveling from New York to Los Angeles by plane. In cases when these client visits support the business, bring true value to the client, and lead to more and better work, business travel is worth the investment. But, as a recurring, weekly exercise used simply to have a few minutes of face time or client meetings, these trips are a great waste of time and energy.

Critical Business Travel

Business travel, at any point during your career, should be viewed primarily as a means of gaining and retaining work. Anything related to travel that allows you to build your business, your expertise, and your list of leads and clients should be pursued without hesitation. Anything related to simply filling a seat and being "part of a team" should be avoided. What may be critical travel in the beginning should quickly turn into nonessential travel as your business grows and your opportunities increase.

You will likely be heavily dependent on travel at the start of your independent business career. Establishing relationships and gaining critical mass in the number of projects you agree to support takes quite a lot of effort and requires a bit of initial onsite time. Weekly onsite trips might be considered critical travel at the beginning of your independent career, because you won't have a project otherwise. However, as you acquire a pool of simultaneous projects, you must relegate weekly onsite travel to noncritical business travel.

There are three questions to ask yourself when determining whether travel is essential:

1. **Is the client better off with me onsite?** The client is not generally the best source to answer this question. You must answer this yourself. You must determine whether your time will be well used while onsite. Are there meetings and discussions that simply cannot take place in a conference call? Are you interacting with appropriate personnel and making progress while onsite? If your answer to these two questions is yes, then pack your bags. Often, a majority of developers travel across the country to sit alone in a cubicle and program. This is not a good investment of your time, money, or energy for anyone involved, but it is the norm.

2. **Is the work I am doing something that can be done remotely?** Writing code and working through the software development life cycle is not usually dependent on location. However, if you are a junior developer or a member of an interactive team, you will find most likely that sitting together with others is a requirement of the project. When you are an expert programmer, coding is best done alone at your site, especially if you are fostering your independence in business.

3. **Is this particular trip affecting other areas of my business growth negatively?** The key here is to travel wisely. Every time you sit on an airplane or spend a week in exclusive onsite time with a client, you turn down other potential opportunities. If you are a "one-project" show—where you only participate in one project at a time—then it is irrelevant where you are. If you want to be onsite, it won't impact your business, because you don't have a business—you have a project. If you are working to prosper in your career, then there is never a time when you will have a single project, and therefore you must always be available to take on additional work and also interact with existing clients. Time onsite with a client should generally be viewed as lost time for every aspect of your business, and therefore travel and onsite time must be capable of significant business impact to make it worth your time.

Rule Much of your ability to code your way to wealth and independence is dependent on your ability to maximize your time and efficiency. You must be able to support multiple projects simultaneously and ensure all your clients feel like they are your top. This balancing act can be difficult to maintain if travel time is cutting in to your work time. Again, travel wisely.

Noncritical Business Travel

Noncritical business travel often consists of traveling to a client site and spending four to five days a week onsite. In general, you are in a staff augmentation role and are there largely for your presence. There may be occasional status meetings and development discussions, but most often you will find yourself alone in a cube programming, or passing the time trying to stay busy.

In a world in which online meetings are available to everyone, global communication is instantaneous, and system development can take place from anywhere, it is surprising that so many corporations still engage in the repetitive onsite staffing model. However, this is the business model for many companies you might support as a contractor or a consultant.

Rule Always consider the nonmonetary costs associated with travel. Travel requires you to give up part of your personal life, and to be apart from your family and friends. It means spending countless hours in airports, airplanes, taxis, and hotels. This expenditure of time and energy may be necessary in many cases, especially when starting on your path to independence, and it is important that you understand the costs to travel beyond money.

During the early days of your career, you need to "do your time"—investing whatever it takes to get things in motion and becoming a viable resource. With time, you need to shed what has allowed you to become successful and begin to move in a different direction. If you are a seasoned professional and you have skills that differentiate yourself from the pack, don't continue to accept onsite staff augmentation roles.

Redefining the Rules

Although noncritical business travel is often a requirement for certain projects, it is certainly not to your long-term advantage, and should—from day one— be something you try to minimize. There comes a time when you must say no to how things are done to achieve growth and progress on your path.

As Albert Camus wrote in *The Rebel*, "What is a rebel? A man who says no, but whose refusal does not imply a renunciation. He is also a man who says yes, from the moment he makes his first gesture of rebellion." At a certain point, you must be willing to refuse to continue to take part in traditional forms of business travel—the thing that made it possible for you to succeed in the first place—and engage in those aspects of business travel that further your primary goals of wealth and freedom.

The essence of being highly successful and independent in the tech field (and in most of life) is working in this way. You learn the game, master the game, and then redefine the rules to continue to engage in the game.

CASE STUDY

A few years into my career, when I was commuting by plane to various projects on a weekly basis, I looked around at others on the plane who were doing the same thing, and had been for the past 20 years. I promised myself that I wouldn't do that when I was their age. My key goals were to eliminate senseless travel and to work remotely, except when there was an extremely good reason to be onsite. I focused constantly on the need to reduce travel and engage at a different level, and I took a variety of steps to make that happen. Combining branding, publishing, business development, and communication changes, I was able to reduce my amount of travel drastically. With thought and willingness to focus on the growth of yourself and your business, you can eliminate noncritical travel.

Seven Techniques to Avoid Unnecessary Travel

Use the following guidelines to avoid unnecessary travel.

1. **Build your business.** With many opportunities occurring at the same time, you won't have the option to travel. If you have a half dozen development projects proceeding simultaneously, you won't be able to step away for a week to sit onsite with one client. Your ability to set limitations on how you engage in your business improve significantly when you don't have to travel excessively.

2. **Be an expert.** Set yourself apart. Through your experience, your professional skill set, your leadership, and your exposure, you can set yourself apart as an expert rather than a commodity. In a pool of resources of equal experience, it is difficult to convince the customer that

you should work remotely. However, if you have enough expertise, and a body of work that validates your abilities and credentials, it's easier to make a case that your clients are better off with you involved, even if it means substantially less face time. As Figure 1-1 shows, the more expertise you have (which equates to value to the client) the less time you should spend in noncritical travel. And as mentioned, eventually, it should be eliminated entirely.

Figure 1-1. Increase your expertise and decrease your travel

3. **Master communication.** Someone who has the ability to communicate effectively and professionally over the phone has a much greater chance of convincing a client that remote work is a viable option. Many coders avoid the phone at all costs, relying on e-mail and other "low-stress" forms of communication. Phone communication, for example, is a learned skill, and should be one of your highest priorities. The ability to make a call, return a call promptly, and communicate over the phone like you are there in person sets you apart from the crowd and allows you to work from anywhere.

CASE STUDY

My first job in the tech field was with the help desk of an Internet service provider. At the time, I was extremely uncomfortable on the phone, almost to a point of fear. My first call was from a subscriber asking how to delete e-mail from his inbox. It was so stressful to me to be on the phone that it took about 15 minutes to understand what he was talking about and then walk him through the steps (highlight and click Delete!) to complete it. Now, 16 years later, my business is heavily dependent on phone communication, and I make or take hundreds of calls a month. Many of my clients I never meet in person, and our work and relationship is sustained through phone conversations over months and years. All communication is a learned skill and requires practice. Never underestimate the importance of the phone in your success and your ability to minimize unnecessary travel. E-mail should be for secondary communications, only.

4. **Stay engaged.** The truth is, most clients want their contractors to be onsite largely to keep an eye on them. Many people believe if someone is "working from home" they cannot be productive and won't focus on the work. Your task is to demonstrate to your client that you are involved, and overly productive. Send e-mails documenting your progress and asking questions, which demonstrates your engagement with the work. Make phone calls to fellow members of your team; offer to assist them and ask for their input. Be engaged. Any number of communications takes substantially less time than traveling and sitting onsite, so be liberal with your involvement, and show that you are highly engaged and indispensable.

▨ **Rule** The most unproductive times are those spent onsite with a client in a staff augmentation role. When you are offsite, your priority is to be as productive as possible, and work through things as quickly as possible. When you are onsite, the goal is to look busy and conform to the culture of the company. In virtually every case, you will be exponentially more productive when working remotely from your own office. The amount of wasted time in the corporate world is astounding, and it doesn't align with the pursuit of independence.

5. **Be willing to prioritize.** I know a number of people who choose to travel on a repetitive basis, not because the business requires it, but because they want to be on the road. In many cases, they have children at home and they want the break. In other cases, they simply aren't taking an active role in determining how their life will play out. They're on the road because of lack of thoughtful planning. If you are using your work to escape from more important responsibilities, or you travel because you don't have a better alternative, you are failing to prioritize. Take the time to identify what it is you want from life, both professionally and personally, and be willing to rank your personal responsibilities over the nonessential demands of your professional life.

6. **Don't fear losing a client.** Being successful and independent means you are not tied to any one client. Although you should always strive to bring value to a project, and want to be seen as a valuable resource, you also must set boundaries. Client demands can be overwhelming at times, and in many cases unacceptable. Clients who demand too much of your time limit your ability to work with other clients and to find new, and potentially more desirable, work. A client who demands constant travel should be viewed as a less desirable client. Part of building your business is the willingness to part with clients that drain your time and energy.

CASE STUDY

I had an excellent remote working relationship with a client, and he was very pleased with my delivery and project execution. One day there was a crisis with one of their internal systems and my customer asked me to come onsite. He wanted me there on a recurring basis, because his manager decided he wanted in-person time with everyone. I told them that I wouldn't be able to support the travel—especially cross-country in the middle of winter. At first they tried to negotiate with me, but when they realized there was nothing they could offer that would entice me to travel, the manager became irate and began to question all the work I had done. Within weeks, I was thrown off the project. This is an extreme case. Most of the time, you will have reasonable clients, and only occasionally will you be confronted with unprofessionalism and negativity. You are your boss; you get to choose with whom you work. Stay firm in your conviction about what is reasonable travel, and know that your value is high regardless of where you sit.

7. **Be clear about your expectations.** Be decisive with yourself about what you want from your business. Write your own ideals of how you want to engage with clients, and how much time you want to spend on the road and onsite. Unless you know precisely what you are willing to do, you won't be able to be true to your expectations. The world will guide you where it wants, unless you are willing to specify what *you* want. After you set your own expectations , be clear with current and potential clients about how you are willing to engage.

A Word on Staying in Motion Mentally

Movement comes in two primary forms: physical and mental. Physical movement in the business world through professional travel is ubiquitous. Business travel is easy to recognize, to witness, and to engage in. Mental movement, on the contrary, is much less common and requires much more from the person engaged in it.

Being in motion mentally means being aware of what is around you, your relationship with your work, your goals for your professional and personal life, and all the opportunities and paths opening around it. Mental motion means being able to shift directions to meet customer needs and the changing marketplace, being open to shifting directions and plans, and working to reinvent yourself on a recurring basis. A constant reflection on your situation, your desires, what you are doing with your life, what you are doing for those around you (client, family, associates, and so forth) is required for you to be mentally open and aware.

To attain your ultimate goals of freedom, independence, and wealth, you must be open minded, dynamic, and opportunistic—willing to go where the path leads. Coupling a strong mental openness with a purposeful approach to business travel will skyrocket you to the top of your profession.

Nine Essential Rules for Travel

Travel should always further your business. Use the following rules to ensure your travel is building your business, not taking away from it.

1. **Network while in town.** Before and during any trip, try to find as many contacts in the area as possible and offer to meet with them. When you travel a long distance, people often find the time to meet with you on short notice. After catching up with what's been happening in their life (be mindful of them, too), turn the conversation to how you might be able to help them. Perhaps you developed something you'd like to share with them, or perhaps it is simply an offer of a free lunch or dinner. Never, however, approach these meetings with the intent of selling something, rather, view this as an opportunity to reconnect. These connections can open opportunities both for you and for the people with whom you are meeting. Approach their success with the same level of interest as your own success, and unexpected positive options will open before both of you.

CASE STUDY

I was planning a business trip to the East Coast and intended to reach out to a number of old clients for whom I had done work in the past. I had just published a new book, so I offered to stop by and meet with them in person and give them a copy of the book. There was client I hadn't spoken to in several years. Just offering to meet with him and hand him a free copy of my book led to a six-month paid engagement. If I hadn't been traveling in the first place, and I hadn't reached out to him and offering something of value to help him with his work, this opportunity would never have opened up.

---

2. **Meet with multiple clients.** If you are doing things right, you will have many sales leads at any given time. While working on multiple projects concomitantly, you should have a half dozen others you are tracking to acquire new business and new projects. Whenever you make an onsite trip—either for delivery or for sales—meet with as many clients (or potential clients) as possible. Let every lead or active client know you are in town, and figure out a way to have an in-person meeting with him or her. This is an excellent way to keep dialogue alive, and to remind people of your existence and the work you do.

3. **Use your travel time to be productive.** When you leave your regular life behind and travel across the country, you'll have a great deal of free time. Sometimes the chaos of travel can be to your benefit. Use your time to do delivery, put together advertising material, brainstorm about how to reach out to new clients, and identify new offerings.

CASE STUDY

In winter 2006, I traveled every week. There were many flight delays and cancelations, and I spent much of my time in the Salt Lake City airport. I used the airport time to my advantage. I did almost all the writing and code creation related to my contributions to my first multi-author book while sitting in the concourse cafeteria.

4. **Consider travel an investment.** In some cases, clients reimburse you for travel, but as your career progresses, and travel becomes more a part of sales than delivery, you are often required to pick up the tab. In the world of IT, you generally charge top dollar for your expertise, and you need to invest in your business travel accordingly. Don't be cheap. Taking the cheapest flights and staying in the cheapest hotels may save you a few dollars, but it cheapens your overall mindset and persona. The energy you put out in the world comes back to you. If you look for the cheapest way to travel, your clients look for the cheapest resources they can hire. Invest (but don't go overboard) in your travel and yourself, and it will lead to better results.

5. **Look professional.** Coders are known for their informality—and some are even known for their questionable hygiene. When you are a smalltime developer or when you work in the privacy of your own office, dress as you please. However, when you travel to client sites, clean up, dress well, and look like a professional. The way you present yourself is key in personal encounters. If you are trying to sell a high-revenue deal, dress and look like you should be paid a high price.

CASE STUDY

I arrived at a client site well dressed, but not as well dressed as the client or other employees. The company required everyone wear a necktie. That night I bought several ties. Here was an air of professionalism I hadn't seen elsewhere. Shortly after I visited them, I went to another client and decided to wear one of the ties. When I walked in, a group of us eventually sat down to discuss the potential project. One of the group members said I needed to remove my tie or the discussion would go no further. So, although it is always correct to dress well, you never can tell what a client might expect.

---

6. **Be ethical.** There is an entire chapter on ethics in this book (Chapter 4). Ethics apply to all aspects of your professional and private life. However, being ethical during travel is something always to keep in mind. There is anonymity in your person and your activities, and there are many negative things that may call for your attention and situations that will allow you to act in any manner. In all things you do, act as if everyone around you knows you, and that all of your activities and , conversations, and diversions were being made public. Treat people like you would want them to treat you, and as if you will see them again tomorrow.

7. **Arrive early.** In general, always try to arrive the night before an important client meeting. Airplanes get delayed, bad weather occurs, roads get closed. The worst thing you can do is arrive late to a meeting, especially after investing the time and resources to get there. If you are in a staff augmentation role where you show up weekly, it is less important to arrive early, as an occasional delay is expected. But when you are planning a one-time onsite trip, invest the extra time to get there well ahead of when the meeting will take place.

8. **Choose a hotel chain.** Most travel perks are irrelevant. Airline miles, it sometimes seems, can rarely be redeemed for anything but free magazines, and the time invested in tracking various frequent traveler programs are a waste of time. However, there is one exception to this: hotel memberships. When you are in business for yourself and you must cover the costs of hotel stays, you'll find that you can easily redeem free nights with any of the major

hotel chains at any time. Saving $200 a night while on a four-day business trip can add up nicely. Combining frequent stays with a hotel-themed credit card for everyday purchases has a sizeable positive impact on your travel expenses. It also ensures you are staying in a professional, clean environment, and you stay focused on the business at hand.

CASE STUDY

I've spent a lot of time on the road, and I have stayed at a wide variety of places. It took me years to come to the realization that I needed to stick with a specific chain of hotels while traveling. The episode that made me never look again at creative housing options occurred about five years into my career. I had forgotten to book a hotel in advance and I ended up in a small city late at night. All the hotels I could find were booked for the night. Finally, around midnight, I found a little motel that had a vacancy. I walked into the room and I realized I had made an unfortunate error. Although the room was dim, filthy, and filled with bad air, I went ahead and spent the night. My sleep was filled with nightmares, something I am never troubled with. I checked out five hours later and never forgot to make a reservation in advance again. There are mistakes that we make in life only once.

9. **Don't use travel as an escape.** I have heard that some people find their sanctuary when on the plane. No cell phones, no e-mail, no pressures from the outside world—in short, a refuge from the demands of the modern world. Some people use travel as their primary escape; they long to be in the air. To me, this is a professional failure. If you want a respite from everything, go into nature, breathe the fresh air, sit on a canyon wall, be alone with your thoughts. If the only escape or the only time to get work done is at 35,000 feet, you most likely need to take a step back and reassess your priorities. Paul Theroux wrote, "You define a good flight by negatives: you didn't get hijacked, you didn't crash, you didn't throw up, you weren't late, you weren't nauseated by the food."[1] If you are defining you travel time by negatives, you are probably on the right track. Be grounded; take control of your life.

---

[1]Paul Theroux, *The Old Patagonian Express. Mariner Books, 1989.*

Conclusion

Travel is critical to your success, but should be done in moderation. Too much time on the road limits your ability to deliver at your maximum capacity; but, too much time in a stationary position reduces your opportunities. Finding the right balance is an art; it requires a thoughtful approach and constant refinement. Successful travel is valuable to both you and the client, and should not be done solely to fill a seat. The cost is too high, both in personal sacrifices and loss of professional opportunities.

2

Skills

Foundations in Programming and Business

> *Those who speak against killing and who desire to spare the lives of all conscious beings are right. It is good to protect even the animals and insects. But what about those persons who kill time, what about those who are destroying wealth, and those who destroy political economy? We should not overlook them.*
>
> —From Nyogen Senzaki's 101 Zen Stories[1]

You have a responsibility to perform at your highest capacity in everything that you do. As you progress along your professional path, and as the years advance, your abilities and capacities will change and your responsibilities will increase. The first step on your path is to build a foundation of understanding and a skillset that will enable you to grow and build a career. After you have built these, you will need to move beyond delivery and begin to create and engage in opportunities at a higher level.

As part of your foundation, you should understand the full software life cycle, and be able to work at an expert level within delivery, testing, deployment, and support roles. Your skillset should also include an extensive base of skills that are not coding specific, skills that enable you to engage in a broad array of project-based work. Throughout your professional life you must constantly expand your skills, your offerings, and your fundamental understanding of the processes and systems at work within organizations and within the world of business.

---

[1]This story can be found in: Paul Reps and Nyogen Senzaki, Zen Flesh, Zen Bones. Tuttle Publishing, 1998.

If you remain in the same job, never advance to the next stage, and refuse to grow, learn, and expand your capabilities and offerings, you not only limit your potential and positive energy but also negatively affect those around you. As the opening quote from *101 Zen Stories* implies, the person who wastes time and resources is guilty of more than just inefficiencies and sloth. Those who seek a job only for security, and never push themselves to higher achievements, will not be able to harness the creative powers of their trade and of business, and will never attain security, let alone independence or wealth.

It is your duty to move to higher levels of functioning in your personal and professional life. To do so, you must understand the nature of the world in which you work. It is critical to see the creativity behind coding, and the nearly limitless possibilities for work and opportunity that this skill creates. It is crucial to understand how to move from solely programming to an entrepreneurial role of forming and managing a business built on coding. This requires that you view business as a necessary, transcendent, and deeply purposeful engagement.

In the following sections, you will explore the nature of programming and what it takes to be a coder who can rise above pure delivery and establish your own dynamic business. You will also look at what the nature of business is, and how you can harness the power of this system. By focusing on attaining a broad range of skills in programming and in business, and by understanding the nature of the activities and systems you are taking part in, you will have an excellent foundation from which you can achieve your aspirations of wealth and independence.

The Nature of Programming

Creativity is at the core of programming. Often, people perceive coders as highly logical, analytical, left-brained; and there certainly are those who fit the stereotype. However, the programmer whose entire focus is on the code and who can't come away from the keyboard is not going to be able to rise above the pack and move toward success and freedom. Rather, it is the programmer who is focused on the bigger goals and is willing to alter his or her approach to work and deliverables that will ultimately move on to greater things.

CASE STUDY

I was out with a group of people one evening, and a woman I had not met before asked me what I did for work. I told her that I was a programmer and that I worked with technology. She frowned. "You looked more creative than that," she said as she walked away.

Programming is a creative exercise, but it is a trade, and therefore ultimately a commodity, similar to any other product or service. One coder can easily be replaced with another, and engaging in the trade alone is only enough to sustain a basic career. Your goal is to differentiate yourself from others so that you are not easily replaceable. The more development skills you have and the wider the range of projects you have worked on, the more valuable you are to your current and future clients. By supplementing your skillset and enhancing your business insight and strategy capabilities, you can set yourself apart from the competition and become someone who clients cannot easily replace or consider to be a commodity.

Programming Skills

Your core programming abilities are what make you saleable and what enable you to engage on projects. The broader your offerings across languages and platforms, the wider the array of job options that will be available to you. You can build a business specializing on one platform, but you must be among the best in your specialty to be successful. The following is a list of technology areas that are common in virtually all environments. The more familiarity (or expertise) you have across these areas, the more valuable you are to clients, and the easier it will be for you to find paid project engagements. You will want to broaden your offerings as you grow professionally, so that you are able to accept any opportunity that presents itself.

Rule Every aspect of coding and platform development is important to master. There are many coders who can write applications but know virtually nothing about databases. There are many systems integrators who can map data and write SQL but have no idea how to write data access layers or other code-intensive components. There are endless user interface and graphic designers, but few of them have the skills to tie the front end with back-end databases. If you lack the ability to deliver across all the various aspects of applications, your ability to constantly grow and expand your project base will be severely limited. You will have no problem finding a project occasionally, but you won't be able to land multiple simultaneous projects, and clients will perceive you as a replaceable commodity. This is not the path that will lead you to your goals.

---

1. **Languages**. You need to be a master of at least one major programming language and be familiar with many of the others. Among your goals should be to deliver a project in each of the major languages at some point in your career. The major languages for which you need expertise and experience include (but certainly are not limited to) .NET, Java, web-based languages (HTML/PHP/ASP.NET), database languages (T-SQL, XQuery), and data languages and formats (XML/XSLT). Many people in the technical field have familiarity with platforms and how to configure and deploy them, but only a subset of those people know how to program in a variety of languages. Mastery of structures and principals of coding is a core skill if you intend to be a technologist in business for yourself.

Rule The businessperson who has expertise in both coding and development is rare. Being among that elite group will give you an advantage in your business dealings, as you will be able to deliver projects at any level. Sales, acquisition of new work, development, testing, deployment, and support are all skills you will personally bring to the table, which means you can discuss at any level with anyone and come to quick decisions at any point in the sales or delivery cycle.

---

2. **Databases**. Knowing how to build a relational database from scratch (tables, fields, relationships, keys) and how to program various database components (stored procedures, functions, and so forth) will be useful on almost all of your projects. Whether you specialize in database-specific tasks or not, your ability to query data and compile reports will be of value to virtually every client. Databases are common to every company. Having expertise with the major offerings in this space (especially SQL Server and Oracle) will be a great asset to you in finding project work.

3. **Platforms**. You should have deep skills in at least one specific platform. Portals and document repositories (SharePoint, for example), CRM suites (Dynamics, Salesforce.com, and so on), and integration applications (such as BizTalk, Oracle SOA, and Sterling B2B) are the types of platforms that are broad enough to build an entire career on. There are endless options for project work in almost all of these spaces, and plenty of areas in which you can specialize.

Rule Specializing on a platform does not mean restricting yourself to working solely on that platform. You must have a generalized skill base. Although many coders work on only a single product for most of their career, this is not a path to a marketable, sustainable solo business built for wealth and independence.

4. **Operating systems.** You likely won't work consistently across all the operating systems, but having basic familiarity with each is a good idea, and having expertise with at least one is essential. This includes the major server (Windows/Unix), consumer (Mac), and mobile (Apple/Android/Windows) operating systems. Demand is greatest for programmers with skills on the server side, as a majority of organizations are running either Windows or Unix-based servers. Mobile and consumer operating systems are everywhere, and there is a great deal of work to be had on these operating systems as well.

Rule Do not adhere religiously to any single language, platform, or operating system. Although you will find most of your work in a specific language, operating system, platform, and/or database, you must never discount or disparage the others. You will have your preferences and your opinions, but refrain from being dogmatic about technologies.

There are many people who are religious in their beliefs about their preferred technologies, and vociferously attack other platforms. For example, open source proponents are notorious for disparaging Microsoft platforms. You are in the business of engaging in income-producing opportunities with a variety of organizations, and you must remain open to the application of many technologies and free of ties to any specific language or platform. The more dogmatic you are about your technology preferences, the further you are from attaining wealth and independence in business.

5. **System diagnostics.** Being able to troubleshoot processes across systems is a skill acquired over time. You need to track and address bugs in your own applications, of course, but you will also have frequent opportunities to troubleshoot systems and applications that you did not design or implement. Your ability to understand how applications are built and to debug various types of architectures is important in any environment, and increases your value.

6. **Basic networking**. Knowing the basics of networking enables you to talk intelligently about issues related to things such as load balancing, network traffic, and large data migrations. Being able to troubleshoot issues related to client connectivity, virtual private networking (VPN), and other common actions required in daily work ensures that you are not wasting anyone's time and are not perceived as novice by the client.

7. **System integration**. Various platforms are used for integration, but you do not need to be familiar with any specific single platform in this space. Rather, you should be familiar with how integration between systems and vendors occurs, and what options, architectures, and platforms are available for building out these integrations. Although having specific development skills in system integration probably is not a prerequisite to your success, your value to any client undoubtedly is elevated if you know how to build out an integration on a specific platform, are very familiar with how different APIs are structured, and understand concepts pertaining to exception handling and retry patterns.

8. **Web technologies**. You should understand the various web technologies and how web-based applications are hosted and made secure. In most of your projects, there will be web components being developed. You may not be directly involved in this development, but knowing how these technologies work and how they need to be configured in various environments will be useful on many projects.

■ **Rule** You need to keep your skills current, and work to constantly expand your offerings and your depth of knowledge. Among the variety of ways to do this, the best is client work with cutting-edge technologies and solutions. See Chapter 3 for more approaches to keeping your skills up to date.

Beyond Programming

Coding and technology implementations are your foundation, but alone these do not allow you to engage at the level necessary to land a wide variety of project work that will enable you to attain true wealth and independence. In addition to coding, you must develop the skills in the following list. You may already have several of these skills, but you must also make sure that you market them as part of your service offering to differentiate yourself from other coders. The coder who can document clearly, participate in business analysis and design, architect a solution, and discuss technical strategies is far more marketable than the coder who can only build software and applications. A list of those skills you will want to enhance your offerings is as follows:

1. **Communication.** A programmer who cannot communicate via e-mail and the phone will forever remain an employee. You must practice and perfect your ability to communicate. E-mails must be concise, effective, and timely. Phone conversations must be natural and businesslike. Nothing is more off-putting to potential clients than amateurish communications.

2. **Presenting and speaking.** Building on core communication skills, you must be able to speak authoritatively on your subject, and be able to persuade people to trust you, purchase from you, and continue working with you. To succeed at the level you are aiming for, you must be able to speak in front of small audiences of IT personnel to lay out options for architecture, and you must be able to communicate with higher-level executives on strategies and implementation approaches. You must be able to present to small groups on development-centric topics and to larger audiences on business-level concepts.

3. **Documentation and writing.** You will be called upon not only to document your work but also to put together diagrams, whitepapers, and other documents that are related specifically to the project work you are doing. In addition, to grow your business and acquire new clients, you will need to be able to write various types of public-facing material (see Chapter 6). You must master the language and its grammar, and become comfortable expressing yourself intelligently through writing. You have daily practice with this through e-mail and similar communications. Use these as opportunities to refine your writing skills so that you can apply those skills to expanding your delivery work and ultimately to growing your business.

4. **Architecture and design.** Your coding and development skills must be at a level that enables you to architect a top-end solution for at least one platform or technology. You should have the ability to design across technologies, and know how to appropriately use various components and platforms.

5. **Business analysis.** Larger projects involve a team of people, generally including analysts who work to define and document requirements. For smaller projects, you likely will have to act as an informal analyst, writing design documents and gathering requirements. Thus, you must be able to mine data from databases and spreadsheets, know how to ask questions of the appropriate people to get solid requirements, and be able to document information in a variety of formats.

6. **Testing and quality assurance (QA).** This is another area of expertise where people specialize and make careers. You will be asked not only to test your code but also to write test cases and document outcomes. You do not need to be a QA expert, which is a full-fledged career itself, but you should know the process and be able to test your code according to various methodologies.

7. **Strategizing.** When working with smaller clients, you will often have the opportunity to strategize and set vision from both a technology perspective and a business perspective. To set strategy, you have to engage on many projects and ensure that your skills are always up to date. Bring ideas to the table that you have seen implemented elsewhere, and that have worked in your own projects and business.

8. **Leadership and decision making.** You will be placed in positions of leadership numerous times in your career. In a team setting, where you are delivering a portion of a project, you will have opportunities to steer conversations, offer options for implementations, and guide people to the most appropriate solutions. As the owner of your company, you will have endless conversations in which you will be asked for guidance and direction. You must have the courage to be decisive, the resolve to act on those decisions, and the ability to lead people to make appropriate choices.

9. **Knowledge sharing.** You will need to train and mentor others, and you will have to perform knowledge transfers on solutions you have built and are leaving with a client to maintain and support. You must be open to sharing your knowledge and able to clearly articulate what you have built and how others can support, maintain, and continue to develop it (in coding or in business).

CASE STUDY

My first programming job was with a small rural ISP. A senior programmer there had worked in the industry for 15 years, and was a genius developer who had built his own commercial fractal software in the late 1980s. I knew virtually nothing about coding, and he would help me by constantly offering code samples and advice. As a novice, I couldn't believe how open he was to sharing his knowledge.

When we know very little, or are insecure in our abilities, we try to keep what we do know to ourselves. When we are confident and generous, we share what we know with anyone who is interested. In some cases you can bill for it, while in other cases you offer it for free, but in every case you do it willingly. The more that you share and the more that you give, the more that will come back to you (see Chapter 12 for more on this).

The Nature of Business

From a microscopic, localized view of business, it can appear very cut-and-dried. In the trenches and the cubicles, the repetitive nature of the tasks can drain the strength and energy from those who pass their lives there. As a programmer, for example, it is very easy to have a myopic view, focusing on the minutia of the tasks at hand and the specific project being delivered. If you have worked only for others and have never created something new on your own, the business world can certainly seem very limiting.

However, stepping back and taking a macroscopic view of business, you discover a system that thrives on ingenuity, creativity, and an energy that is greater than the individuals and organizations that it comprises. It is this creative and energetic system that you will be part of as an independent businessperson.

As you step into independence, you will experience firsthand how very different the role of an entrepreneur is from that of popular culture's soulless businessman. You will unleash the underlying energy that attracts clients to you when you take actions that are seemingly inconsequential. You will see how your thoughts have a direct impact on the opportunities that present themselves to you and the income levels that you can achieve. You will find an almost supernatural system that enables you to attain virtually any goal you create for yourself, as long as you are willing to put in the effort, work through the processes required, and keep a healthy mindset. Business is a system that both sustains those who seek only a paycheck and are ignorant or disinterested in its power, and elevates those who embrace its essential nature and wish to attain great levels of success for themselves and those around them.

Factors for Success

According to Matthew 13:12, Jesus said, "For to the one who has, more will be given, and he will have an abundance, but from the one who has not, even what he has will be taken away." There is a fundamental truth in the world that those who are successful become more successful, while those who are not will fall even further. The rich become richer, the poor become poorer, sometimes due to human factors, sometimes due to environment, but ultimately due to laws of nature that are as real as the law of gravity.

Certainly, there are baseline skills and principles that will make your path to success, wealth, and independence easier, such as a business-friendly environment, personal intelligence, hard work and dedication, and skills that are in demand in the marketplace. Additionally, the power of positive and creative thought will ease the path—a firm resolve to gain success, a tireless devotion to attain the goals that you have set for yourself, and a fearless persistence to achieve those goals.

Rule Intelligence is helpful, but is not a requirement for success. There are coders of varying degrees of intelligence with different traits and backgrounds. Extremely intelligent people are often handicapped by their views and visions, while people of average intelligence can amass great fortunes and create great change in the world. By taking certain steps, having solid skills, and implementing specific patterns that have been proven before them, anyone should be able to attain success with coding as a business.

Ultimately, though, what must be present in your life beyond these important principles and activities is the unerring and timely ability to alter course based on the environment and the market. You must be able to change your mind, your offerings, your engagements, your approaches, and your prices instantly as opportunities appear and as the world around you changes. Having a specific strategy in mind about what you want to deliver is good, but you must go where the market leads, follow the openings that are before you, and say yes to everything positive that presents itself.

"And so when occasion requires the cautious man to act impetuously," wrote Machiavelli in the The Prince, "he cannot do so and is undone: whereas, had he changed his nature with time and circumstances, his fortune would have been unchanged." You must be able to react to what is happening around you, and alter course as part of your overall strategy. For example, position yourself as an online service provider rather than as a web developer; the former is a generic, ever-changing role, while the latter is a specific delivery for a specific medium. "Online service provider" easily enables you to move from one type of work to another, while "web developer" pigeonholes you in a single space. Make sure you are able to change with the times and are constantly updating your views and skills based on where opportunities around you are directing you, and you will almost surely guarantee your success.

A Word on Luck and Chance

It is a common inclination for all of us to attribute the great successes of others to luck and chance, and certainly luck and chance do play a role in our successes and failures. "I returned and saw under the sun, that the race is not to the swift, nor the battle to the strong, neither yet bread to the wise, nor yet riches to men of understanding, nor yet favor to men of skill; but time and chance happens to them all," wrote the troubled philosopher of Ecclesiastes. There are intelligent people who never rise from the gutter, there are wise men who suffer poverty. Many people are born into negative, oppressive environments or countries from which no escape or freedom is possible. Much of this is chance circumstance, and constitutes factors beyond one's control.

Although it is certainly true that not everyone will be successful or have the opportunity to live in an environment in which wealth and independence are options, it is absolutely true that everyone can be successful within the confines of the life they are living. It requires a combination of beneficial circumstances (which a person can create around them), strong skills (which a person can learn, practice, and master), and a strong mental attitude (which is entirely within the control of the individual). If you are living in a business-friendly country where freedom exists and the pursuit of a trade is an option, you have the chance foundation upon which you can largely control your future success, mediocrity, or failure.

■ **Rule**   Although luck and chance are dynamics in all areas of life, attaining a level of success that enables you to reach your goals of wealth and independence is almost entirely within your control. Assuming you put in the time, have the necessary skills, and have the ability to focus and execute on your goals, and your environment does not preclude you from being able to engage in industrious and profitable work, the opportunity to pursue and attain wealth and independence is yours.

From Programmer to Entrepreneur

Realizing that wealth and independence are yours if you want them is the first step in enabling yourself to make the leap from programmer to entrepreneur. Opportunities will open before you the moment you decide in earnest that you want to make the change. For the growth and success of your business, and the attainment of wealth and independence you are after, there are a wide variety of skills to develop and activities to engage in. The following list gives a breakdown of the essentials, while the remaining chapters in this book give details on each of the key areas.

1. **Have technical aptitude.** If you have the interest and the aptitude to learn and code, you can choose whether to remain purely in the role of developer or to have success as a businessperson. A good developer is someone who has the capacity to learn new technologies quickly. If you are not able to learn new platforms and languages easily, you will fail at being an independent businessperson. Being a successful entrepreneur within the fast-changing world of technology is partially dependent on your aptitude to acquire and apply new skills.

2. **Have confidence in yourself and your skills.** The quickest path to failure is lack of confidence in yourself, while the quickest path to success is the presence of that confidence. You must be very confident in your current skills and have the capacity to embrace the acquisition of new skills. Many extremely talented and intelligent people never enter into independent business because they lack the confidence to do so. There is no excuse for low self-confidence, and if you suffer from it, you must do everything in your power to seek outside help to elevate it. Low self-confidence will severely limit your ability to attain independence and wealth.

3. **Have confidence in the system.** You must trust the system. The system comprises the processes and methods of the economy and business itself—how work is created, how opportunities surface, how the exchange of capital occurs. Capitalism and the associated methodologies and support systems have existed and prospered for much longer than your career will last, and you must trust that their principals work and will remain steady into the future. You have to believe that advertising and marketing create leads, that networking and positive communications close leads, that an abundance of work is available for anyone who wants it, and that the more you participate, the more opportunities that await you. Believing in the system and fully engaging in the activities that have worked for others before you is often a difficult shift in thinking from being an employee, but one which is necessary to achieve success.

Rule   If you want to prosper in business and attain wealth and independence through it, then you must be willing to embrace the ideas and systems that sustain it.

---

4. **Be aware.** Always know what is going on across all your projects and all your business transactions. Stay on top of leads and potential opportunities, following up frequently. Stay in communication with all your colleagues across your various projects. Know what you have committed to, and keep those commitments. Talk with subcontractors and employees, and know their ambitions, strengths, and weaknesses. In everything that you do, stay alert and be present.

5. **Be willing to walk away.** Not every client is worth retaining, and not every opportunity or lead is worth pursuing. If you have only one or two clients, you are going to feel pressure to satisfy their every need and to do everything possible to preserve the status quo and extend your work with them. If you have many clients, and so much potential work that you can't deliver on all of it at once, you are going to be less inclined to accept projects that are not of interest to you or from a client who is less than desirable to work with. If you are hungry for work, work is often meager. If you are satiated with work, more work will come.

6. **Ask rather than tell.** You may be a listener or you may be a talker, but you have to put aside your tendencies and become someone who asks rather than tells or remains silent. Your goal as a businessperson is to find ways in which to help others, and in turn have them pay you for your help. To help clients, you must find out what they need help with. In some cases, a client will know that they need assistance in specific areas. Generally, this assistance is in the form of development or architecture for a specific function of their business. To truly help them and expand the relationship, you must ask questions to find out whether they are struggling to find solutions in other areas, and, if so, then offer assistance. Ask a person about their challenges, and you may be able to offer advice and become a trusted long-term advisor. Asking questions will uncover opportunities for work where none existed before, while talking relentlessly will likely close a door of opportunity.

7. **Be willing to change your thinking and your approach.** Always be open to new ideas, be willing to defer to others, and be prepared to go wherever the market leads you. Your offerings should change as you grow in skill and as the technical world around you advances. You and your business should be dynamic, ever-changing entities, going where opportunity and goals direct you. As Confucius reportedly said, "they must often change who would be constant in happiness or wisdom." You must often change if you want to be constant in the success of your business.

8. **Give rather than receive.** In all of your interactions, think about what you can offer to others rather than what you can gain from them. Don't view potential clients as sources of income for you, but as opportunities to provide your services and expertise to someone who needs them. If you have something of value, share it with another. If you see something you can help out with, offer your help. Make it a practice of offering to help, and the money will follow.

9. **Invest in others.** Acquiring wealth and independence in a service-based industry requires that you work within a broad community, and that you value and take interest in others around you. Your path will be lined with people who will assist you in attaining your goals, and you need to view them as valued companions in your professional journey. You also need to think of ways to help them improve their professional situation, and ask them what you can do to assist them. Send people work. In many cases, the people with whom you work will prosper on their own and go on to higher-level positions within companies that could use your services. If you have shown an honest interest in them, and have given them something in the past, they are likely to share their successes and opportunities with you.

Conclusion

Your ability to write code is the foundation to advancing to your highest capacity of professionalism. Expanding from this basic learned skillset and broadening your skills to be able to deliver quickly and successfully on multiple platforms and in multiple languages, all while immersing yourself in the creative energy available to the developer, will enable you to master the art of coding. As a master of this skill, you then need to move into more business-focused activities, especially around communication and architecture. As you continue to mature in your skills, you will more easily transition into a business-centered role, where delivery is only one of your many offerings. To reach your highest potential, you must also develop the skills necessary to succeed in business. With a complete technical and business skillset intact, the systems and processes are in place for you to achieve great success. A great deal of work is involved, but the path is clear for you to attain your goals of wealth and independence.

Discipline and Education

The Importance of Continuous Improvement

An investment in knowledge always pays the best interest.

—Benjamin Franklin

Discipline and education are integral to your ability to achieve the type of success necessary for true wealth and independence. Your strength of character has everything to do with your ability to succeed as an independent businessperson. There is no company to hide behind and no anonymity when dealing with clients. Your presentation, your ability to understand and be understood, to act professionally, and to execute on tasks all depend on your character, and your character is made directly from your education and your self-discipline.

Discipline

A strong discipline gives you the framework within which to learn, deliver, grow professionally, and achieve your goals. There are both physical steps to be taken and metaphysical thought patterns to be established to allow this discipline to take shape and impact your professional life. This dualistic combination of concrete and abstract approaches will allow you to set yourself apart from others who are in the same profession, and will enable to you build yourself into someone who is able to act at the highest level and step away from the mundane, everyday existence of mediocrity.

Eleven Steps for Professional Discipline

The following steps can be practiced to acquire the basic professional discipline you'll need to be successful with the concrete aspects of your work.

1. **Rise early.** As a developer, you can code at any time. As a businessperson who also happens to be a developer, you will find your days are often consumed with high-level discussions, sales, meetings, design sessions, and so on. As your success and the number of opportunities you engage in increase, the time that you will have for delivery work will decrease—during business hours. You must set aside a period of time during which you can get your work done—uninterrupted development time. There are some people who argue their best time to work is in the evenings, but they are generally not the people who are independently successful and wealthy. You will find very few truly successful coders who start their workday at 10 AM and wrap up at midnight. Rather, it is the very early risers who seem to find success and are most able to use their time wisely. In *Meditations*, Marcus Aurelius wrote, "In the morning, when you rise unwillingly, let this thought be present: I am rising to the work of a human being. Why then am I dissatisfied if I am going to do the things for which I exist and for which I was brought into the world? Or have I been made for this, to lie under the blankets and keep myself warm?"

■ **Rule** If you do not engage in work in the early hours of the day, it is very unlikely you will gain the level of wealth and independence you seek. You must be ahead of everyone on all your projects before true business hours commence if you want to be able to make progress throughout the remainder of your day. Business hours for you should allow for ample time to generate more business, take phone calls, and deal with nonprogramming-specific work.

CASE STUDY

I generally start my day at 4:30 AM. There is nothing easy about waking up early, but I know that if I don't get an early start, I'll fall behind at work and will have difficulty in being productive (which means more work at a later time). I code, write, and plan for the day during these hours when it is rare to see others online. If I am working on a project with offshore resources, I may schedule a meeting to talk with one of them, but generally I try to keep these early hours for activities that require focus. In a couple of hours in the predawn hours, I can often accomplish a full day's equivalent of work. By the time most people start their workdays (between 8 AM and 9 AM), I have already completed most of the deliverables I'll need to produce for that day. I can focus on meetings, sales activities, and customer communications throughout the regular workday. I generally wrap up mid to late afternoon, and reserve the evenings for other activities.

2. **Dedicate time.** No matter where you are working—a home office, an office downtown, a shared space with colleagues—there will be distractions and items calling for your attention. In general, business hours should be spent at business activities, even when things may be slow. Your ability to force yourself to be dedicated to your work will determine your ability to attain the types of wealth and independence available to you. If you have no development work to do, consider it a rare opportunity to focus completely on marketing and generating new business. There should never be downtime at the office, especially when there is no billable work.

3. **Dedicate space.** Your office is your space. Don't think you can achieve independence and wealth without an area dedicated solely to your work. You can dedicate virtually any space, but it must be professional and conducive to work. A basement corner with stale air, bad lighting, and constant background noise, or a corner of a bedroom is not appropriate working space. If you are going to work out of your house, you must have a room used solely for work—one that is separate from all your living activities and one that allows for professionalism (no background noise during calls, for example). If you are going to work from an office apart from your home, ensure your commute is short and your expenses are minimal. Don't waste time getting to and from work. You are independent and free; don't add a commute to it.

4. **Respond promptly.** When an e-mail arrives, respond to it. If it is going to take a while to complete the tasks outlined in the e-mail, let the person or group know you are working on them and specify the general time you'll deliver. When a call comes in, respond to it as quickly as possible. There should never be a time when an e-mail or a call is not responded to promptly—usually within a few hours or at least during the same day. Only in rare cases is it appropriate not to respond immediately.

Rule   This is worth repeating, and you will see it throughout this book. Responding promptly may be the single most important discipline for the independent businessperson. The individual who picks up the phone when it rings or responds instantly to e-mail or voice messages is the person who will walk away with the business. Not only is it a sign of advanced professionalism and an avenue to gain and increase your income and clients, it will actually reduce your overall workload. Staying on top of communications and responding when they arrive allows you to deal with things in the moment, rather than stack them up for dealing with later, in a more inefficient manner.

CASE STUDY

I've known many clients who take weeks or even months (!) to respond to e-mail and phone calls. In one case, I received a response to an e-mail six months after I sent it. These calls and e-mail messages were all related to business at hand, and were not personal requests or solicitations for additional services. It always amazes me on several levels when someone doesn't respond right away. The question that stands out most, however, is how people are able to get anything done, or how it is possible even to remember to reply to something weeks after its arrival. The massive amount of wasted time and effort in responding to old business and communications is inconceivable.

5. **Work efficiently.** Make sure your working environment and equipment supports your ability to work on multiple tasks and projects at once. For example, many of your clients will require that you VPN onto their network. In most cases, you can only connect to one VPN session at a time on a single machine, which means you are limited to a single task. Work with multiple computers and surround yourself with a desk setup that allows you to turn quickly from one computer to the next. Dual moni-

tors, multiple computers, wraparound desks, and good phones (you need both landline and cell) will ensure your hardware and environment will support your need for multitasking. You must learn to be able to bounce between projects rapidly, doing a deployment on one while updating and compiling code on another.

Rule Invest in your equipment and your environment to ensure you have everything you need to work in the most effective and efficient manner possible. Purchase top-of-the-line laptops so that you can remain mobile, in case you need to take your work on the road. Have dual monitors on each of your machines.

---

6. **Set priorities**. Naturally, your clients will always consider their work the highest priority. You have to be able to determine for yourself, across all the work on the table, what is the highest priority at any given moment. You want always to deliver on time or ahead of schedule on all your tasks, which means you must be able to look at all the aspects of the various projects and understand what takes precedence. By communicating expectations with your clients, you will have a great deal of flexibility in how you deliver, and will be able to juggle multiple high-priority tasks.

Rule Never talk with your clients about your other projects or priorities. You must not share your stress or your work with anyone but yourself. Remain ambiguous with clients; they should know they are not the only ones you are working for, but they should never know specifics about your work or what you are working on at the moment, unless it applies specifically to them.

---

7. **Stay positive**. There are many things that can bring negative reactions: too little work in the pipeline, too much work in the pipeline, difficult client relations, difficult project work. There are endless opportunities for complaint and discouragement. It is your challenge to put stressful situations in their place and maintain a good attitude regardless of what is occurring. There will always be times for stress, and there is only so much you can do about difficult situations, but you do have control over your view of things and the words you

speak. Bad-mouthing clients is something that may not jeopardize your success when you are an employee, but a self-employed person should eliminate negative talk and thought, and always be thankful for the work that is available. Negative thinking is the quickest way to experience failure.

Rule Your thoughts influence your world. If you look at a client situation negatively, chances are high it will remain a negative environment. If you alter your thinking and look at it with a positive spin, chances are high it will turn into a different situation. Always remember the significance of your thoughts and outlook on what happens in the physical world around you.

---

8. **Set boundaries**. Clients and work will consume all of your time, if you let them. Certainly, there will be times in your career where you will have to work long hours, but this should be in your control, not at the whim of others. You are providing services and availability to your clients and your projects, but you are not there to be abused. You must be firm in your boundaries and communicate your availability. If someone wants more of your time, you can give them options for when you will be available.

9. **Identify personal time**. You must have a time when you can step away from work and focus on other aspects of your life. If you start early in the day, wrap up work by mid afternoon. Don't work weekends or evenings, except in rare cases when a deployment or a conversation is required. Figure out how to deliver more efficiently, and don't allow work to cut into personal time on a regular basis.

10. **Keep code simple**. In business programming, you are working to get tasks done, not to write the best algorithm or the most efficient process. You always want to develop the best architecture you can, but you must be able to figure out how to deliver things in the most simplistic manner possible. Not only will this allow you to get things done more quickly, it also allows you to hand it off more easily to the next person. Forcing yourself to keep things simple is an important discipline for the business developer.

11. **Keep a list**. List the things you need to do. Don't keep them in your head. When you are one project, it is reasonable to think you can keep your to-do list in mind. But, when you have multiple things to do, and you are taking calls while writing code for several clients all at the same time, you must jot things down on a to-do list or your stress will mount, you will forget tasks, and you will fall behind.

■ **Rule** One of the best ways to manage your time effectively is through the use of a task list. Place a stack of Post-It notes on your desk. As tasks come up—in e-mail, on the phone, while doing development—write them down. Check them off as you complete them. Throw the notes away as you finish the tasks. Although this strategy is extremely basic and simple, it will have an enormous impact on your time availability. It also gives you a sense of accomplishment as you check items off the list.

Six Activities for Mental Discipline

It is told that the Buddha said, "To enjoy good health, to bring true happiness to one's family, to bring peace to all, one must first discipline and control one's own mind. If a man can control his mind he can find the way to enlightenment, and all wisdom and virtue will naturally come to him."

Mental discipline is the most challenging discipline there is, because it is entirely within your control. Your success or your failure is completely your own. Investing time in the various practices listed next will improve your mental discipline. A powerful mental discipline will allow you to excel at virtually anything you do, and will have an immediate and direct impact on the success of your business. The following activities will increase your mental discipline.

1. **Listen**. One of the most important aspects of mental discipline is limiting your talk and practicing the art of listening. The world is filled with noise, and there are many who speak, but few who listen. Learning to listen will increase your understanding of those around you, allow you to reduce the amount of time you spend in meetings and discussions, and improve your ability to retain clients and build your business. Improving your listening will also improve your coding; your efficiencies in communication will improve, and your code will become more simplified. Ask those around you if you are a listener or a talker.

Many people believe they are listeners when they are not. "A dog is not considered a good dog because he is a good barker. A man is not considered a good man because he is a good talker," said the Chinese mystic Chuang Tzu.[1]

Rule Be constantly aware of your words and be respectful of everyone's time. There is so much time wasted and energy drained in the world by people who talk in excess. In the corporate world, the garrulous nature of people expresses itself in a culture of meetings and wasted hours. Things that could be said in a few sentences end up taking hours of time with multiple participants. When meetings with a group of listeners take place, the meeting will last for five minutes and will result in many actionable items. When meetings with even a single talker take place, nothing is accomplished in an hour, and generally the meeting will run long.

---

2. **Seek solitude**. Step away from the noise of the world. Turn off and unplug. Go out into nature and be alone. Solitude is critical to your pursuit of independence and to your ability to have a disciplined mind. Independence is inherently a separation from those around you, and the truly independent person knows the value of solitude. Many find no time to reflect on their lives and the roles and activities they are investing in. Without time to reflect and to examine, growth is slowed and goals are difficult to achieve. As Socrates said in Plato's *Apology*, "the unexamined life is not worth living." Without solitude, there can be no self-examination. Without self-examination, there can be no understanding of purpose. Without purpose or creativity, your pursuit of wealth and freedom will be fruitless. You must constantly define and redefine what your goals are, what your dreams are, and whether the steps you are taking professionally and personally are getting you closer to your goals. Solitude is a crucial component for your success.

---

[1]Herbert A. Giles, *Chuang Tzu*. Routledge, 2013.

3. **Exercise.** In Chapter 13, we examine health and exercise in more detail, but note here that recurring and regular physical exercise is essential to the calm and orderly mind. Set aside time each day to walk, run, or otherwise engage in movement outside. Fresh air and movement are necessary for a healthy mental state.

■ **Rule**   Your physical exercise can be an activity that allows for solitude and reflection, and ultimately an inward focus on the interior life. Running, walking, and bicycling are all activities that can be pursued alone, and allow you to get away and have time to yourself. Going to a gym doesn't allow you to escape the noise.

---

4. **Show temperance.** The sober mind has a far easier and sustainable path to success than one that contends with temptations. You must decide what your priorities are in this life—if pleasure and sociability, then state it; if freedom, wealth, and independence, then state it. There are many cases when material wealth is bestowed on the drunkard and the glutton, but true freedom can only be had with a clear mind and clear body. If you wish to attain your goals, and those goals include operating at your highest potential to achieve the health, wealth, freedom, and purpose that belong to you, then you must look honestly at your views on alcohol, food, drugs, and other consumables that have, throughout history, caused many to fall. Someone who practices mental discipline will find there is no place for the disorder brought on by these substances.

5. **Be fearless.** It is easy to become fear based. Worrying about whether there will be work next month is one of the most common fears in business. You have to distance yourself from these common fears and assume the best instead. Assume you will have more work than you can handle. If your pipeline is diminishing, take actions to increase your business rather than worrying about what might come to pass. In client discussions, tell the truth as you see it, without fear. As an independent businessperson, you are going to need to control your fears, and the controlling of fear is a practice. The more you practice, the better you will become at controlling it. Your success depends on this, and it is a discipline you must take part in.

6. **Study**. You must study and educate yourself. The rest of this chapter outlines in detail the various approaches to education you can take in both your professional and private lives. Constant study within and external to your trade is important, and will ensure you are continuing to grow and expand mentally.

All these activities increase your mental discipline. With a disciplined mind you will be able to live a full and purposeful life. A strong physical and mental discipline is the foundation from which you can be successful at whatever you choose. Having looked at the various aspects and activities related to discipline, we now turn our focus to the various types of education that will supplement your ongoing growth.

Types of Education

There are three primary types of education that you will engage in that will impact your career growth. The first is traditional education—university degrees, master's in business administration, and other forms of continuing and higher education. The second is professional development—on-the-job education, courses on new platforms, developer conferences where new ideas are introduced, soft skill classes (such as communication and negotiation skills), and professional certifications. The third is your personal education—reading, mentoring, and thought growth. For you to be able to separate yourself from others and excel at what you do, you will need to engage fully in all three of these.

The first is open to anyone and is required to enter into the workforce. The second method is followed by a certain number of career-oriented individuals who want to be active, stay on top of new technologies, and stay relevant to prospective employers by showing something on a résumé. The third is engaged in by a fractional subset of anyone in the tech industry or otherwise, and is the single most important form of education to set yourself apart and allow yourself to operate at your greatest potential. True success, wealth, and independence will only come to those who practice all three of these approaches to education.

Traditional Education

Higher education in all its forms falls under traditional education. Undergraduate, graduate, master, and doctorate degrees are outcomes of traditional, formal education. After you have started your career, there is little value in continued formal education if your goals are independence and wealth in the technology industry. Investing in a master's degree may allow you to climb the corporate ladder, but it will impress no one when you are working directly with clients.

Rule Most people who are interested in purchasing your services want to know you can get work done; they are not looking for degrees or certifications. If someone is focused on your educational credentials, what schools you went to, what letters appear after your name, then this person is most likely either someone in human resources or someone who is very low on the corporate ladder. In either case, this is most likely someone who actually cannot buy your services.

Formal education is important when you have nothing else to show. If you are a 22-year-old with no job experience, you need an undergraduate degree to prove you can complete something, and that you have the basic skills required to learn and focus. If you are a professional who is planning on becoming independent, you should already have plenty of real-world experience that is of interest to your potential clients. Formal education should be a thing of the past for anyone pursuing independence and freedom through business.

Rule Don't put too much stock in formal education. A college degree is certainly a critical path to your ability to get hired at the beginning of your career, but beyond that it has little value. Adding credentials after your name may allow you to rise up in an organization, but if you are independent, they will have no value. Focus on your skills, your delivery, and your professionalism, and leave higher education for your youth.

CASE STUDY

It was very early in my career, and I was riding to a company meeting with a guy who had been hired around the same time I had. He told me how he had attended an Ivy League school, and his degree had allowed him to land this job. Within a few weeks, the company we worked for went through a massive layoff (it was early 2001) and he was cut. I remained employed. I had a college degree from a small mountain school in Colorado—a true second-rate higher education. Tuition cost $1,200 a semester. When it came time for layoffs, no one looked at our degrees; they looked at our skills and our ability to deliver on paying work.

Professional Education

There are many forms of professional training and education that should take place throughout your career. These include the following:

1. **On-the-job training.** Everyone, when they first start a project or a new job, engages in on-the-job training and education. This is pedestrian, and should be an expectation for anyone who is actively engaged in life. With technical work comes learning—forced upgrades of technology, the application of new code to solve problems, constant peer reviews, architectural reassessment of deployed projects. At least, that is what should be happening. Often, as you look around a corporation, you'll find people sequestered in their cubicles doing the same work they have been doing for years, struggling with the same problems they have in the past, and still not mastering the technologies that have been present and unchanging since before they began working there. As an independent business-person, you should always be aware of changes that are taking place in your client's environments and always be several steps ahead of all of them in your understanding and application of technology.

■ **Rule** Strive to work with the most current platforms, and to know previous versions. Most of your clients will not have the latest operating systems and platforms; the corporate world is slow to change, and it is costly to move through upgrades and migrations (especially for operating systems that impact users outside of IT). When a client asks about issues related to migrations on platforms that you are working on for them, you should be able to talk intelligently about them. If you are not current and the client knows more about migration paths than you do, you will quickly find the client no longer has a need to have you around.

---

2. **Courses.** It is common for employees to be told to participate in week-long (or longer) training on plat-forms that may be new to the company. This can be an acceptable way of education, but it really is better for the employee rather than the self-employed. These courses are time-consuming, which means during this training time you will not be able to work on any of your deliverables

for clients. These courses are also expensive. Generally speaking, as a self-employed businessperson, there are far better ways to ramp yourself up on technologies than to force yourself to attend a deep-dive training class. The best use of your time is to take a few hours to learn about a technology and ramp yourself up on the basics of how to work with it so you can understand when and how to apply it. Then, find a client who needs something implemented using this new technology.

Rule If you truly want to learn a technology, you must develop something on it for a project. Be familiar with all technologies that may be applicable to the clients you are working with and the types of projects you are delivering on. Try to learn new platforms and technologies as part of the projects you engage on. Learning them as you apply them to real-world solutions will be a far better use of your time and a quicker way to understand them than by participating in any sort of professional-level training course.

---

3. **Developer conferences**. Going to group conferences is useful to you as an independent businessperson in only one way, and that is if you are a speaker or presenter. If you are going to attend, or if you are going to network, save your money and your time and generate business elsewhere. If you are going to present or to speak, go with the intention of meeting people who need your services. Conferences should be treated as potential ways to generate business, but not as viable educational opportunities for the self-employed.

4. **Soft skills development**. Any opportunity to advance your soft skills through classes, newsletters, online seminars, audio books, or similar methods should be invested in. In general, these are low-cost ways to keep your mind thinking about ways in which to connect better with people and to increase your ability to provide services and communicate. Chances are your ability to negotiate, sell, persuade, and engage are far weaker than your technical skills. Invest in your business skills at a rate equal to or greater than your investment in technical skills.

5. **Professional certification.** There is some limited value in professional certifications when you are independent. If you are working to gain traction in a specific technology that you do not have project-related experience on, then certification may allow you to move into that space. But, the amount of effort required to gain certification is generally far greater than any work that may be gained from it. Certification is primarily for the person seeking employment from others. As an independent technologist, you should be part of the teams that are creating exams for others to take, rather than taking exams to prove you know the topic.

Personal Education

As an independent businessperson, you are your business. Investing in your business is investing in yourself. Educating yourself improves your business. The most important thing you can do for the growth of your business and for your own growth is to have a lifelong devotion to personal education. Although there are endless pursuits that can potentially lead to personal education, there are two primary activities you can engage in that will allow for constant personal growth and business expansion: the first is reading; the second is being mentored.

Reading

Very few people who shaped the world we live in were not readers. The literate are the most able to make changes because they have been exposed to the most ideas. If you want a dynamic life built on independence, and you want the ability to think and advance, spend time with books and with the great minds of the present and the past. Novels and fiction are fine, but works of history and ideas are those that will enable you to climb the ladder to success and independence most easily.

Nineteenth-century German philosopher Arthur Schopenhauer wrote, in *The Art of Literature*, "without books the development of civilization would have been impossible. They are the engines of change, windows on the world, 'Lighthouses' as the poet said 'erected in the sea of time.' They are companions, teachers, magicians, bankers of the treasures of the mind. Books are humanity in print." If you are not constantly reading, you cannot be a thought leader, and you will have a difficult time in becoming independent and wealthy.

Rule   A life without reading is a life that doesn't change. Many people who are interesting and changing in youth stagnate in adulthood because they have no external ideas to keep them fresh and to keep them thinking. A constant flow of ideas from books will keep you relevant and thoughtful, and will facilitate achievement of your personal and professional goals.

Mentorships

The most impactful change you can bring to your business through education is by engaging in a mentorship. As a solo independent businessperson, you do not have many people to talk to about ideas, and no one who can hold you accountable. A mentorship, if done properly, forces you into a different role, and allows you to communicate with someone who is in your business and doing similar things as you. Early in your independent journey, you will benefit greatly in working with a mentor who has built a highly successful independent practice. Later in your career, after you have achieved relative success, you'll likely want to work with mentors on specific aspects of your business.

Rule   Choose your mentors wisely, and work with different ones throughout your career. You will see results beyond your expectations.

The act of engaging with a mentor can transform you and the work that you do. Professional mentoring is expensive by design. The goal is to have you put enough money into the relationship that you take it seriously, and that you value the person you are working with. The person who is mentoring you has taken years to get to where he or she is in a position to help you, and can cause great changes to take place in a very short time. Though expensive, being mentored will pay dividends well beyond your investment, as long as you have clear objectives and are willing to listen to and act on direction.

CASE STUDY

Working with my first mentor allowed me to double my income within six months. He laid out steps that he thought were important, and I followed each of them—even ones I saw no value in. I developed content and created a more professional online presence. By investing heavily in my professional life, I was greatly rewarded. By listening and acting on the advice of someone farther up the ladder than I was, my business was transformed and I reached the goals I had specified at the beginning of the engagement with this mentor.

A Word on Education

Lao Tzu, in *Tao Te Ching*, wrote, "Learning consists in adding to one's stock day by day. The practice of the Tao consists in subtracting day by day: subtracting and yet again subtracting until one has reached inactivity." Your focus on education is building up and expanding your knowledge base, but at the same time you must set aside what you have learned to get to a place where you can progress to the next level of your business and your learning.

There is a dichotomy in the idea of education and improvement. Often, the more educated a person becomes, the more distance is placed between that person and the fundamental ways in which nature works. Academicians are well known for their aloofness and separateness from the world. So, too, is the saint or monk, who through deep reflection ends up in a state of pure inactivity, focusing on the infinite. Businesspeople who aim for the highest levels of success, though, must act on both of these simultaneously—educating themselves while at the same time subtracting what they have learned to allow for greater achievement.

As you build your level of expertise, you will become more proficient in your work, ultimately to a point where you, as Lao Tzu notes, will be inactive (or have the potential for inactivity).

If, for example, you were to continue to do the same thing you did at the beginning of your career, you should (if you are aware, interested, and learning) be able to come to a point where you can complete in a day what once took you a month. Assuming nothing around you changes, this leaves a substantial amount of time during which you have nothing to do. In a traditional employment situation, this is often the case; the longer people stay in their positions, the more time they must work to stay busy (or to look busy). In private practice, all times that allow for inactivity can be used for building your business and furthering your goals.

Conclusion

There are many people who want money and freedom without having to do the work. What you must know as a person working toward financial freedom and independence through coding as a business is that hard work is part of the process. Eventually, you will be able to enjoy the fruits of your labors, but first you must labor. Your labor will lead you more readily to wealth and independence if it is done in a disciplined manner, with ample education throughout your career. The more serious you take this discipline, and the more time and energy you invest in education, the more quickly you will be able to achieve your goals. Discipline and education are lifetime commitments, and cannot be done overnight. Take your time, acknowledge where you are, and set your sights on where you want to be. Continue to refine yourself and your manner of work until you see the results you require to achieve your goals.

Ethics

The Foundation of Relationships and Business

Whenever you do a thing, act as if all the world were watching.

—Thomas Jefferson

The ability to act ethically and to work for a good outcome for everyone involved is the mark of a truly successful individual, and paves the way toward your goals of freedom and prosperity. You are confronted daily with determining right actions and establishing trust. Investing time to ensure you have a strong foundation for ethical behavior—in your personal life, professional life, how you code and how you deal with others—is an immensely beneficial activity, and it is a core requirement for achieving true wealth and independence.

Virtually every interaction in business is based on trust—trust in the process and trust that the rules of engagement are followed by everyone involved. For the vast majority of interactions and transactions, this trust relationship stands, and those who engage in business abide by these rules. In cases when the interactions follow a pattern that has been set, such as in a simple exchange of money for a product, the rules are simple and it is easy to determine the appropriate action. However, as you move down the path of business independence, you will encounter many scenarios that are unique and for which you don't have an immediate answer for how best to proceed. In all cases, you must be able to determine what the most appropriate action is.

The ethical businessperson is, by necessity, an individual who thinks and who conducts constant self-review. By living with the guiding principal of doing everything "as if all the world were watching", and by careful study of yourself, of your motivations, and of those around you, you'll be certain you are taking the appropriate steps to work in the most ethical manner possible.

▓ **Rule** At the foundation of your success is your character. An ethical character creates success that leads to abundance and opportunity for everyone involved—you and everyone you encounter. A character based on deceit, immorality, and lack of virtues leads to success that may appear attractive on the surface (fame or material gain, for instance), but behind which lies a trail of pain, loss, and destruction for everyone involved—you and everyone around you.

The Transitory Nature of Morality

In a society in which right and wrong are relative, and morality is considered to be something of personal choice—where the evils of yesterday are elevated to the good of today, and people are applauded for the very acts for which they were reprimanded yesterday—it can be debated whether appropriate personal and professional behavior is dependent on the situation, the day, the culture, or your mood.

▓ **Rule** To be morally and ethically relativistic is to walk the common road. To take the high path, and live and work at your greatest potential, you must constantly examine, challenge, and refine your core beliefs, actions, and ideas. There are fundamental truths and correct ways of living and interacting, and it is up to you to search these out and understand them.

The challenge of determining the right action has been an ongoing subcurrent of the human drama. In *The Journey and Ordeal of Cabeza de Vaca*, which is a first-hand account by Alvar Nunez Cabeza de Vaca written in the 16th century, the customs of the native Mariames tribe are described. For fear of marriage to a potential enemy, tribesmen rarely allowed a girl to live. "They cast away their daughters at birth; the dogs eat them." So, too, they would kill the majority of their sons, if told to do so in a dream. These customs, although looked at by other cultures (then and now) as diabolical, were regarded among that specific tribe as both moral and acceptable, and even ethically responsible.

There are endless examples throughout time of people who engaged in customs that we can identify immediately as morally void and ethically lacking. Cannibals lived in a society that embraced and revered the practice, American plantation owners had slaves, and the common man throughout history despised and killed Jews. At each of these times, people deemed "good and honest" by those around them engaged in behaviors that others in different time periods would say were ignorant, foolish, and wrong.

What society says is good is not a measure of good, and what society says is wrong is not proof of something being wrong. You have to be able to step away, study, think, and be willing to know what is right and wrong, regardless of political correctness, the judgment of others, and the whims of the age in which you live. A careful study of history, philosophy, and religion may aid you in this endeavor, but ultimately you must be willing to stand on your own.

An independent businessperson, whose wealth is self-made, must be willing to be stand alone in thought and action. True independence comes with a recognition of eternal truths and adherence to rules and behaviors that have governed the conduct of men and women throughout time.

Fundamental Ethics of Behavior

Underneath the current of political shifts, cultural divides, and relative truths, there is a longstanding tradition of fundamental rules of behavior, of morality, of ethics. These truths date back through the ages and across cultures, and define the ways in which we deal with one another socially. Business exchanges are one of these key interactions.

Study is critical. If you want to become a master of something, turn to the masters to teach you. The foundations of truth and ethical behavior can be found in the ancient teachers, philosophers, and religions. If you were planning a year-long expedition to a foreign land, you would fare far better if you were to read guides and descriptions from people who had been there before. As you make your journey into professional success, so, too, will you fare better if you study those who went before you.

In our current culture, we disdain what is old and think those who came before us were simpletons, closer to the apes than we are today. There is talk that we are constantly improving, that a Golden Age awaits us. These ideas are based on a misguided understanding of the nature of humans. The future is not always better, and current minds don't necessarily know more than those of the past.

In actuality, our ancestors had great wisdom, and they should be turned to in matters that are fundamental to how we function in this life. Business has been around since the dawn of humans, and the rules that outline ethical behavior date back to the mists of antiquity. Make a practice of reading books of ancient wisdom—famous philosophers, ancient thinkers. You likely won't achieve your full potential unless you are willing to spend time with the great minds of the past.

■ **Rule** You will not always succeed in taking the most ethical path. Perfection in anything is not possible, but striving for perfection is. As a professional working to achieve the highest level of functioning, you must always work to determine the right actions, but failure must be an expected part of the process. As Marcus Aurelius wrote in *Meditations*, "Do not be disgusted, discouraged, or dissatisfied if you do not succeed in doing everything according to right principles; but when you have failed, return again, and be content if the greater part of what you do is consistent."

There are several questions you can ask yourself in all situations when determining appropriate and ethical action. They are as follows:

1. **What am I basing my behavior on?** All of us have mentors. We learn from every encounter around us— individuals, groups, speeches, books, television. Those with which and with whom you spend your time are those that influence you, consciously or subconsciously. During the course of a week, determine who is influencing you by determining with whom or with what you are spending time. Are the individuals around you positive, thoughtful, and open-minded, or do you spend your time in crass conversation with small-thinking people? Do you spend your free hours doing something that builds character? Or do you spend time doing something that promotes detrimental thoughts and actions? Whatever you surround yourself with and whatever you have exposed yourself to in the past combine to create your behavior and judgment. Review the things and decide whether they further the pursuit of your goals.

2. **Is this action in line with how others are acting?** Anytime we part with how things are done traditionally, we must do so with deep awareness and constant review. The standard flow of society around us has many aspects that should be avoided, and it takes work to understand where we should part from the norm. So if we part from the way of others, we should be very aware of the reasons why, and make sure we do so for appropriate reasons.

3. **Is what I am doing defensible?** As you chart your own course in business, there will be times when the right next step is not obvious, and there will be no one to discuss with or help you to determine the appropriate action. You must decide for yourself what direction you will take and how you will handle the situation. In situations when there is no precedent, ask yourself: If I were placed before a judge, a jury, a set of peers, would my action be defensible? Would I be strong in my conviction of having done this? If you cannot defend your actions in your imagined setting, then you have not come to a viable solution to your situation.

Rule   On occasion, new ideas and ways of viewing the world and our activities in it are brought to light. Revolutionaries, sages, prophets, and geniuses can help us change the way in which we perceive the world and the rules with which we engage. However, in the vast majority of cases, the rules of conduct should be followed. If you find yourself acting in ways that don't align with those who came before you, especially in the case of ethical behavior, you should be very cautious.

The Ethics of Business

In virtually everyone there exists at the same time a strong desire to be successful and wealthy, and a strong distrust of those who are successful and wealthy. Power of any nature breeds jealousy, envy, fear, and suspicion in those who see it. There are many who distrust businesspeople because they distrust the system—primarily because they do not have the strength or will to be part of it.

As you walk the path from programmer to businessperson, you must be aware of the changes you are going through and the changed perceptions of those around you. You can't be too concerned with the thoughts, comments, and criticisms of your peers, but be cognizant that judgments are being made and actions are being scrutinized. You must be able to apply this awareness to all aspects of business, which include the following considerations.

1. **Billing and fees.** Are you being just in the way you come up with your fee structures and how you bill for your work? Chapter 9 includes an expansive discussion about fees and appropriate ways to engage with a client. Always keep the best interests of all parties in mind—your client, yourself, your subcontractors—in all that you do in relation to billing and fees, and you will come out unscathed if your ethics are questioned.

2. **Attainment and alignment of skills.** Having current, cutting-edge skills and knowing the technologies with which you work is paramount. Countless projects have been managed and worked by people who have no business doing so. Numerous solutions have been coded by developers who have no skill in the coding languages being used. Align yourself and your skills properly on projects, and be open and honest about your experience. This is the most appropriate and ethical way of working on a project. (In many cases, clients want junior programmers to work on projects, but they never want a junior programmer to act as a seasoned architect to design their solutions.)

3. **Use of wealth.** As you make your money, be aware of how you are using it. What are you investing in? What causes are you furthering? You should have your own personal objectives of how to donate a portion of your income. Whether to a church, a secular charity, or private causes, a portion of your income needs to flow to others without the expectation of getting anything back. Chapter 12 has information on considerations of how to use your wealth.

4. **Business relationships.** In your various encounters with people in your professional life, always work to aim for the best interest of all parties. Never approach a situation with a desire for personal gain, but rather with the mind-set that all of you may have something to offer each other. Keeping in contact, meeting for lunch, discussing opportunities, all of these activities—even when you are doing them as part of your sales process—should always be pursued with the specific goal of furthering the business relationship and working for a positive gain for the people with whom you are meeting. Approaching a situation with the sole intent of trying to get a paid engagement from it is both rude behavior and a poor approach to the ethical treatment of professional relationships.

5. **Employees and contractors.** You will likely find yourself employing others, either as traditional employees or as contractors. The goals you set for yourself (independence, wealth, and so on) should be the goals you set for others. If you are engaged in lucrative work, those you bring to the table should also be rewarded and engaged in lucrative work. Treat your colleagues like you treat yourself, and you ensure they are going to benefit in many ways from working with you on your various projects. Be generous, pay well, and trust people to deliver at their greatest ability.

6. **Yourself.** Treat yourself equally well. Many people have no difficulty considering themselves first, but these people are bores and are troublesome to be around. Most professionals consider their clients first, often to their own detriment. Be ethical and kind to yourself or the system breaks down. Developers are notorious for "ghosting" hours, saying it took 40 hours to do something that actually took 100 hours. They want to stay on target and prove the task can be done within the limitations specified. The problem here is that no one will ever know the original estimate was grossly under budgeted, and there is no way to correct the inaccuracy the next time. Be honest with yourself, fair in the time you charge for, and fair in the amount of time you work. Many people who are self-employed are extremely unkind to themselves. One good test to determine whether you are being ethical to yourself is to look at what you require of yourself and ask whether this is how you would treat an employee. If the answer is no, you must change what you are doing.

The Ethics of Coding

There are four main ethical principles that relate to the delivery of technical architecture and development. These values include writing code that can be maintained and extended easily by someone else (coding for the next generation); ensuring you deliver code based on the priorities and requirements of the project, not on personal preferences (focusing on project and client priorities); delivering the best possible solution within the given circumstances (delivering the best possible solution); and working to provide clients with insights into how to make their solutions better and their business more effective—whether related directly to your immediate project or to the larger picture (being a strong communicator).

Coding for the Next Generation

Some of you may be familiar with the idea from the Constitution of the Iroquois Nation that "in every deliberation, we must consider the impact on the seventh generation." Applying this maxim to coding means everything written should be done with the next person in mind. Unless you are planning on staying with a single company for years, it is guaranteed that someone else will come in and take over where you left off.

Anyone who has written a line of code has inherited a project from someone else. We all know the feeling of looking through a piece of work from those who had no idea what they were doing, and implemented something in such a way that the code has to be rewritten completely. We also know that we have written code that was handed off to someone else and should never have been written in the first place. As a professional, with experience behind you, always keep the next person in mind. Some of the basic ideas of coding for the next generation include the following:

1. **Write code and solutions simply.** There are many ways to write code, and your options change as your experience increases. However, in every situation and at every skill level on your journey, always work to deliver the most simple and well-thought-out code as possible. If a solution to a problem can be coded at the level of an elementary school student or at a PhD level, code at the elementary level. Thinking of the next person means writing at a level that can be understood easily by virtually anyone who picks it up. In general, business programming is about getting a solid solution in place, not about algorithms and efficiencies.

CASE STUDY

I was part of a large, 20+-person team tasked with developing a health-care based solution. The project we were brought in to work was extremely complex and consisted of a variety of cutting-edge technologies and software development kits (SDKs). I likened the solution to the temple of Angkor Wat in Cambodia—incredibly intricate, artistic, and complex; the product of an extremely bright mind, but virtually unusable and unable to be maintained. The same solution could have been built by two or three people in a much more simplistic way, saving the client millions of dollars and reducing the delivery time drastically. The original architect of the solution had missed many of the fundamental requirements of an ethically responsible solution, and the company would pay for this mistake for a long time to come.

---

2. **Document code and solutions thoroughly.** Documentation is often an afterthought, and many times it is not even budgeted into a project. However, putting together simple design and architecture documents, and ensuring your code is documented inline requires little additional effort and should be part of every coder's deliverable. Taking a minute here and there to document what you are doing properly saves a great deal of time for the next person who has to work with your code, and helps minimize the chance that your well-designed and well-executed code won't be thrown out for a rewrite because no one was able to tell what it was doing.

3. **Target deliverables and architectures toward appropriate technologies and skill sets.** Write your solutions to use technologies that are well understood by as many technical resources as possible. When designing your solution for a specific client, first learn about who will be supporting it after you are gone. If their internal team is well skilled with SQL, but knows little about .NET, then build your solution in such a way that it uses database components and functionality rather than writing everything in compiled code. There are cases when you won't have an option in how you write the code, but the vast majority of situations allows for you to design and build solutions tailored toward a certain skill set and technology.

4. **Determine whether what you have written is something you could understand one year from now.** When you roll off a project, you generally immediately forget everything you did. As the weeks roll by, the memory fades. Six months later, a client calls and asks for a bug fix. It takes time to ramp back up, remember what you did, and address the issue. As you write your code, think to yourself: Will I be able to remember what I did here? Is there anything additional I can do to make this easier on myself when I have to revisit it? If you write code in such a way that makes it easy for you to maintain and remember, you make it just as easy for the next person to take it over.

Focusing on Project and Client Priorities

When you are hired by a company to architect and develop a system integration, it trusts you will build the most appropriate solution to match the situation. The priorities of the project are generally clear, but they always center around the betterment of the client, not around ulterior motives that individuals on the team may have in mind. Engaging ethically on a project means you place the client's best interests before your own. If there is work that needs to be done, that is the highest priority. If there is a critical bug that needs to be fixed that is holding up production, that is the highest priority item for you and it must be addressed.

Every client you have should be your top priority, and focusing on all of them at once is a necessity. No client should ever be aware of other work or other priorities you might have. You can do this with the appropriate equipment, skill, mind-set, and working environment, as long as you know how to manage time and as long as no single client abuses your availability.

■ **Rule**   Avoid excessive meetings. It is important to be available virtually any time someone needs you, so limit meetings to an hour or less, and always let your client know before the call that you have a hard stop at the end of the meeting. Be extremely efficient with your time. If one client consumes too much of your time, you are not being ethical to your other clients.

CASE STUDY

I was doing a code review of a product that a developer had recently written and released into production. The code was a custom application that was a core process and integral to the success of the client's product line. The application was massively over complex, and was something that no one other than the developer could ever work with. I asked the developer why he had done the code this way and his answer was "job security." His take was that if he designed something only he could work with, the client could never let him go. The only way that someone could take over this code in the future would be for the company to invest in a full rewrite of the solution. This kind of behavior is very common; people want to own their domain, and they often create (consciously or not) solutions that have been built in a highly unethical way. Deliver top-quality work and lay no claim to territory that others have paid you to develop.

Delivering the Best Possible Solution

You will likely find yourself supporting projects on which you are not the architect and don't have control over how a solution is implemented and supported. In this case, you are often working in a staff augmentation role, and are not considered for consulting or guidance. You may be required to write code that doesn't match what you consider to be good code or a well-designed solution. In cases when you find yourself required to build a solution with which you don't agree, you have two options:

1. **You can walk off the project.** In extremely rare situations, the architecture and solution are so poorly thought out there is nothing you can do to make progress. You will know this at the very beginning of a project, and you need to make a decision on whether you will engage before any real expenses have been incurred by the client. If you know the situation is hopeless—in general, because of lack of management—then it is your duty to let others know why you can't engage and then quickly excuse yourself. Be aware, however, that quitting a project hurts you and the client financially, and is an option that should be undertaken only at times when staying on would be in everyone's worst interest.

■ **Rule** Always strive for the most correct action in a set of given circumstances. For example, assume you find yourself in a situation in which you have very limited time to complete a solution. Coding it by your standards may require two weeks of time, but you only have two days. The number one priority in this situation is to get the work done within the two days; therefore, the most correct action is to come up with an approach that solves the immediate business need.

---

2. **You can express your concerns, use your expertise, and make changes where possible**—all while making progress with the core solution. This approach is sensible and models our situations in life. We live in an imperfect world and are able to make limited changes in this world. Taking this approach in your business life ensures you are constantly seeking to make the best changes the circumstances allow for any given context.

Being a Strong Communicator

The ability to communicate your status, your impressions of the project, and your perceptions and recommendations at a business level is a very important aspect of your overall capability to engage ethically on project. When you are working on a solution, you will be asked the status of the project, how close are you to being done. You must be able to state with clarity and precision the current status, the task on which you are working, any holdups you foresee, and what you need others to do to proceed. The ability to communicate your status clearly and effectively at all times is the most ethical skill and behavior you can have. Countless dollars and unimaginable time have been wasted because people are unable to communicate their status properly.

CASE STUDY

A colleague of mine from China was asked, as developers frequently are, how the project was coming along and what the status of his deliverables were. His response to each question about each specific deliverable was always, "Done." The project manager was pleased with the progress, and the meetings went on like this throughout the course of the three-month project. As the project neared the testing phase, this colleague was asked to move his solution to the quality assurance environment. He replied that it wasn't ready to test. Days went by, and the project manager began to get stressed and upset.

"You told us that this work was done! Why can't you roll it out to test?" he asked.

"In China, we have 30 words for 'done.' The code is 'done,' but it is not 'done done,'" my colleague responded.

In the end, we had to rewrite the code from scratch, because what had been written was neither "done" nor done properly.

Would a code review have helped here? Certainly. This is a perfect example of when a code review would have saved time and money. But the real thing that would have helped would have been professional communication. Knowing how to communicate your status effectively and accurately, regardless of the specific questions being asked, is key to being able to engage in an ethical way.

Dealing with Unethical People

You will meet, work with, and work for unethical people. Many people knowingly do what is wrong for their own gain or motivations; others do it unconsciously. The vast majority of people are simply playing out their lives and are directed, not by any true thought on their own part, but rather by the winds of ideas and incidents that occur all around them. "Man is asleep," said G.I. Gurdjieff as quoted by P. D. Ouspensky in *In Search of the Miraculous.* "Awakening is possible only for those who seek it and want it, for those who are ready to struggle with themselves and work on themselves for a very long time and very persistently to attain it."

Knowing that most of those around you are not fully conscious of themselves and their environment, and are acting at various levels of mechanical thought and motivation, is something you must accept in many situations. Often, you know the heart of people within the first few minutes of dealing with them. You have to make a decision from the start regarding whether you choose to engage in business with them. Individuals who show themselves to be foolish, cruel, deceiving, foul tempered, and mercurial during your initial encounter continue to be so in the future. You must consider all your dealings, deliverables, and interactions in relation to this knowledge and weigh the risks of engagement.

■ **Rule**   Thieves and liars can be charismatic and have enjoyable personalities. Be willing to see the true nature of the people with whom you are dealing, and make appropriate business decisions based on this understanding. If you rule out working or engaging with people with questionable attributes, your world would become very small very quickly.

At times, depending on goals, current work pipelines, finances, and other considerations, it may make sense to engage in risky projects with questionable people. The desire to help is deep within most of us, and knowing we can do the job being requested is often enough to make us want to help anyone who asks. Just make sure you work to assess the true character of people in the very beginning, and plan your work based on the known risks. You may be disappointed in the final outcome, but you won't ever be surprised.

CASE STUDY

Bill was the president of a company I worked with out of New Jersey. He was a man given to his passions, and his emotions were never controlled. I had been hired as the next in a long line of people to update his solution and add new functionality. The solution itself was complex in that there were no well-defined project requirements, but the real complexity was in the personality of Bill. I knew from the first day we met that he was going to be difficult to work with because of the way he talked about and treated people who had come before me. However, I had the skills to be able to help him and I felt that it was possible to make a positive impact through my involvement. There were several of us involved in this project, and I set the price structure at a level that would make the work worth the risk.

We worked with Bill throughout the course of a year. The tasks were getting done, and things in general were going well. Bill went out of his way to express his joy in our work and indicated how extremely happy he was about everything. Whenever he praised our efforts I cringed, because I knew that one day he would turn on me, just like he had on his previous vendors.

One day it happened. Something completely unrelated to the project happened to Bill (relationship? unexpected financial trouble? bad digestion?) and he directed his anger at me and my team. Within days I knew my project with him was over, but unfortunately he owed me about $25K in unpaid fees. Throughout the coming weeks, I tried to save the situation, largely to recoup the outstanding fees, but all my efforts were for naught. I was the ex-girlfriend and Bill had moved on to a new lover.

The project ended, I was out $25K, and I had experienced an excellent lesson in the ways of thieves and unethical people in business. However, ultimately I knew from the beginning that I was working with someone who would turn on me; I had weighed the risks and engaged knowing what would eventually happen.

Conclusion

James Allen in *As a Man Thinketh* states, "A man is literally what he thinks, his character being the complete sum of all his thoughts." Ultimately, you must be thoughtful in all interactions. What you do in your personal life affects your business life. What you do in your code affects current solutions and future developers. Acting honestly in private matters brings honesty to your business. Writing solid code and communicating your status accurately have positive impacts on those working with you and on those for whom you work. If you are serious about your pursuit of wealth and independence, be ethical in the way you live, the activities you pursue, and the way you interact with people.

Structuring Your Business

Taxes, Insurance, and Protecting Yourself

I have already said that a Prince must lay solid foundations, since otherwise he will inevitably be destroyed.

— Niccolo Machiavelli, *The Prince*

This chapter outlines the specific steps required to create a business entity that enables you to engage with any person or organization. It also identifies the various types of insurances policies you should procure, the taxes you should be prepared to pay, and the infrastructure you should have in place. This chapter helps you structure your business quickly, so that you have an entity through which you can start soliciting business and billing almost immediately. Obtaining insurance and addressing the various other considerations necessary to protect your business will take additional time, though you should make sure everything is in place as early in the process as possible.

Structuring your business properly not only creates a legal separation between your personal and business assets, it also enables you to grow, to pay taxes appropriately, and to be perceived by clients and others as a true professional entity. Remember to keep it as simple as possible, to do it as quickly as possible, and to make sure you have a professional, legal, and fully incorporated entity before you start sending invoices or working to acquire clients.

Protecting Yourself

There are some basic precautions to take while structuring your business. As you become more successful, you will become more of a potential liability to yourself. From a liability standpoint, you have little to worry about when you have no assets, because it is unlikely that someone would perceive any advantage in trying to sue you for damages if there is nothing to collect. But as your income rises and you engage in more projects with more clients, the chance of encountering someone who wants to take something from you increases. You should set up your business structure to protect yourself at various levels of income, and you should always carry professional and personal insurance.

The first step in protecting yourself when starting your own business is to form a limited liability company (LLC) through which you conduct all of your business. The second step is to acquire the basic insurance coverage that you need for your current income level and the types of projects you are engaging in. The third step, once you attain a high level of income, is to convert to an S-Corporation. Each of these steps is outlined in detail in later sections in this chapter.

The basic protections that an LLC affords are those common to all other incorporated business entities, and operating as an LLC essentially keeps your business debts and transactions separate from your personal finances. In theory, this means that if your business can't pay its debt, then you cannot personally be held responsible for that debt. It also means that if a business sues you, they will have a more difficult time making a legal claim to your personal assets. The truth is, however, if you are a solo businessperson and your business is failing, you are likely failing personally. In this case, your assets are most likely very minimal and of little interest to others or of concern to yourself. Therefore, the protection from debt collectors is a minor consolation.

The issue of greater concern is the client who sues you and seeks to collect damages from your personal assets. As a sole proprietor LLC, the IRS may perceive you as being separate from your business for financial purposes, but when it comes to a court reviewing and interpreting all the facts, you want to make sure you have the greatest protections possible. When you are generating a high income, you need to take the extra step of electing the S-Corp status for your LLC and carrying professional insurance in order to provide further proof that you and your business are distinct entities.

You never want to operate from a position of fear when engaging in business, but you should take basic steps to protect yourself from the potential disgruntled client who suddenly has a problem with the work you are doing.

Additionally, you should always keep your business transactions and dealings completely separate from your personal dealings. The remaining sections in this chapter outline the steps needed to create your LLC, insure your business and your person, and pay your taxes appropriately. With some basic precautions in place, a strong structure, and an honest and ethical practice, you should feel confident and fearless in your business dealings.

Business Structure Options

You are an independent service provider in technology. There really isn't an easier type of business to create and maintain. If you were manufacturing a product in a shared company, you would have additional considerations regarding taxes and shareholders. If you were a lawyer or medical professional, you would need to have various licenses in order to do business legally. As a coder and service provider, you only need a bit of cash and a few minutes to get your business set up and ready to go.

There are five basic types of entities to be familiar with:

1. **The unincorporated sole proprietorship, or DBA ("doing business as").** This is common for self-employed individuals with limited assets and liabilities, but it is not appropriate for a business whose goals are professionalism, wealth, and independence. There is no value in operating as an unincorporated business, and most companies won't do business with you as a service provider. It is lazy and limiting. Don't consider this as an option for you.

Rule   Nothing will make you look more amateur than doing business as yourself, or DBA ("doing business as"). Take the time to understand how to set up your own business. If you can't demonstrate that you can work through the process of setting up an official entity, you won't be trusted to help out with higher level engagements. You will forever be a one-project show, and will likely only be able to get work through close friends and family.

---

2. **Limited liability company (LLC)**. Your focus should be on the LLC. It is simple, versatile, and flexible. A sole proprietor LLC provides a basic separation of you from your business, keeps your taxes very simple, and eliminates any payroll or other paperwork complexities. It also is a structure that will allow you to convert to an S-Corp quickly and easily once you achieve a high level of income, hire employees, or need to establish additional protections. The LLC is a unique entity, but as a sole proprietor LLC your taxes are passed through to you as an individual, and the separation from your personal assets may be difficult to guarantee except in cases of taxes. It is a great structure for the early years of your independent career, but you will need to look at an S-Corp election as your business matures.

▇ **Rule** When you start out, if you are making less than $500,000 profit in a year and do not have employees, set up a sole proprietor LLC. If these circumstances change, take the S-Corp election for your LLC.

3. **S-Corporation (S-Corp)**. An S-Corp is a corporate entity that allows you to easily employ yourself and others, if necessary. The taxes and paperwork are more involved than for a simple LLC, and the structure makes sense only if you are making a substantial income or if you are employing others. An S-Corp further strengthens the separation of your own financial affairs from your business's, which means your personal assets should be protected from any liabilities that may be incurred professionally. As the IRS states, S-Corps are "considered by law to be a unique entity, separate and apart from those who own it." If you start off with a simple LLC, you can easily elect an S-Corp status at any time.

▇ **Rule** It is simple to perform an S-Corp election within your LLC. However, it is extremely difficult to convert back to a simple LLC once you have taken the S-Corp election. Wait until you are highly profitable and have a reason to pursue the additional advantages of an S-Corp before you upgrade your LLC to have the S-Corp election.

4. **C-Corporation (C-Corp)**. This is the formal corporate entity, and there is absolutely no reason why you, as a solo practitioner or the owner of a small boutique software or consulting firm, would ever want to choose to have a C-Corp. Back in the 1980s, prior to the advent of LLCs, there were some tax advantages to having a C-Corp. Now, there are only disadvantages, and it is an inappropriate structure for what you are pursuing. Double taxation on profits is the primary reason to avoid this structure, while complexities related to administration and tax preparation are strong secondary reasons.

5. **Partnership**. There is no reason why you should set up a partnership in your company structure. If you want a friend, keep them separate from business. If you believe you are lacking skills that would prevent you from being successful as an independent business, work to acquire those skills before you start your business. If someone you are considering partnering with has high business acumen or a set of technical skills you are in need of to land a client, talk with that person about engaging in a temporary contract role rather than as a partner. Although there are many scenarios in which a partnership makes sense in various industries, your goals are to establish and maintain independence and to increase wealth. These goals are more easily attained in a solo practice without partners or employees.

Creating the Business

As the preceding basic synopsis makes clear, you should begin with an LLC, which will be taxed as a sole proprietorship. You will have very little paperwork to administer your LLC and your taxes will be extremely simple. If you make a profit, you keep it, and you pay yourself whenever you want using simple distributions, and without the overhead of payroll. You will pay estimated quarterly taxes, and you'll spend about 15 minutes a year in administration of your company. You'll have a basic separation between your personal and business assets. Most importantly, you will have a structure that any business anywhere in the world can easily work with.

Once you are generating high revenue or need to hire employees, take the S-Corp election in your LLC. Although you will have to do additional tax paperwork, you will be able to save some federal tax payments on standard withholdings (see the sections "Taxes" and "Payroll" later in this chapter). Here are the steps to create your business entity:

1. **Select a name.** This is yours to select, but it has to be unique within your area of operation, which is usually by state. Come up with something professional. Make sure it is a name that allows for a varying number of people within your organization, as you may occasionally hire subcontractors and employees. "Group" is nice to include in the name, as it allows for more changes behind the scenes than, say, "John Doe, LLC."

■ **Rule** Don't deliberate too much about the name of your business. Some people struggle with the name and delay creating their business structure for that simple reason. The name doesn't really matter, as long as you are comfortable saying it.

---

2. **Create your LLC.** Most states allow for the creation of LLCs through the Secretary of State's website. For a nominal fee, you can sign documents online that make your entity official in a matter of minutes. You enter the name you want, and assuming it isn't taken by someone else already (a good thing to check when you are brainstorming your names), you simply enter your mailing address and other information and pay the small fee, and your documents are immediately filed online.

■ **Rule** Set up the business entity yourself. There are plenty of lawyers who can do this for you for a very low fee. However, knowing how to do this yourself ensures that you understand the entire process of setting up a business—something every business owner should know.

CASE STUDY

When I first started my business (Inotek Consulting Group, LLC), I did everything online at the Colorado Secretary of State website. It took about 15 minutes to confirm that the name was unique and sign the online forms. It initially cost $50 to register everything, and costs a recurring fee of $10 a year. The name of the company came after brainstorming with my wife during a five-day, 500-mile bicycle tour of the Rockies.

3. **Get an EIN**. As a single-member LLC, you have the option to use your Social Security number, but getting an Employer Identification Number (EIN) has a number of advantages and is extremely simple to do. Among the advantages, an EIN provides further separation between your personal assets and your business, it looks more professional on tax documentation, it gives an air of authenticity to your company, and it allows your company to engage in payroll activities more easily. It used to take weeks to get an EIN assigned, but now you can get one online in a matter of minutes. You will often be asked to provide a W9 to organizations you are doing business with. Your EIN will be used on these W9s to identify you and your business.

4. **Set up a business banking account**. Once you have your articles of incorporation (which will be printable after you complete step 2) and your EIN, you can take your paperwork to a bank and set up a business account.

That simple four-step process is all that is required to set up a legal business entity. You are now ready to bill and pay taxes.

Taxes

As you make progress on attaining your wealth goals, your tax burden will increase. Your burden will be high, and you have some basic considerations to take into account to ensure you comply with your legal obligations. Overall, your structure is extremely simple, whether you are an LLC or an S-Corp, and there is only a little variance in the tax you are liable for (Medicare is the primary example, as outlined shortly). There are some additional options related to saving for retirement, as discussed in the "Retirement Planning" section later in the chapter, but otherwise you will find that there isn't much you can do to keep more of your money other than to engage in more billable work. The following list gives some brief considerations to make with the various taxation levels.

■ **Rule** Track every business expense and keep all receipts. Your expenses for travel, subcontractors, office equipment, utilities, office space, professional training and development, books—in short, virtually everything business related—are tax deductible. Overpaying your taxes is not something you ever want to do.

---

1. **Federal taxes.** You must pay federal income tax, along with Social Security and Medicare taxes. You pay income tax on everything that you make, but you pay Social Security tax only on the first $117,000 you make. You pay Medicare tax only on salaried income or simple distributions. The only tax burden that you can lighten at the federal level is the 2.9% (as of 2014) Medicare tax. In a simple LLC, all of your distributions would be taxed this additional 2.9%. However, if your business is an S-Corp, you are considered an employee, so only your salaried income is taxed for Medicare, while your additional profit (above and beyond your salary) is not taxed.

Rule You have to pay yourself a reasonable salary when your business is an S-Corp. Your profit is taxed differently than your salary, but the IRS expects you to pay yourself a "reasonable" salary, which means it must be based on what others are making in a similar employed position. Coder's make a wide range of incomes, but you need to base your income rate on the highest possible employed rate. You can do your own calculations, but you will find that $240,000 is at the high end of salaried positions, and is what a coder could make on a full-time, single-project job over the course of a year. Therefore, a realistic "reasonable" salary for you would be $240,000 a year. That means anything you make over this amount is profit, and would be taxed differently than your salary (essentially, you wouldn't pay the 2.9% Medicare tax on this additional profit).

---

2. **State taxes.** Paying state income tax is required in most states, though a few states do not have this tax. You can control to some degree how much you spend on state income tax by living in a tax-friendly state. If you want to move your primary residence to Texas, for example, then you don't have to pay state income taxes. Compare that to doing business in California, which has a 13.3% state income tax rate in 2014.

3. **Other taxes.** You also need to consider sales tax, property tax, and other similar types of taxes imposed by state and local governments. You have some control over what you pay here as well, as how much you pay depends on your purchasing and property acquisition habits and where you reside. If you plan to expand into your wealth, and acquire property, then you will pay these types of taxes with frequency; the government will collect more from you as you broaden your base.

Some people make it their mission to base their living situation on minimizing their tax payments. For example, they might choose to reside in Washington, which has no state income tax, and do their shopping in Oregon, which has no sales tax. You have the opportunity to make a great deal of money, and you can work as hard as necessary to gain the level of wealth and independence you are after. Live where you choose, and where it best suits your nature and your goals in life, and pay the taxes that are appropriate.

Understand that the government will figure out a way to get what it wants from you, and minimizing your burden in one area will generally increase it in another (for example, Washington has no state income tax, but property taxes are higher than in many states.) Recall the advice Jesus Christ gave on taxes: "Give unto Caesar what is Caesar's." Your approach should not be to avoid taxes, and certainly never to complain about them, but rather to pay what is required and figure out ways to make more money. Work harder and faster, and you will attain what you are after, regardless of what the state decides to take back from you.

■ **Rule**　It makes sense to consult with professional tax advisors about payroll and taxes. Although you should be able to do all of your administration yourself, tax preparation and similar things are so tedious and time consuming, or require such specialized skills, that you ought to pay someone else to do them. You can hire a company to do your payroll and take care of all your S-Corp paperwork for a nominal yearly fee. Prices vary, but $250 a quarter should cover every payroll scenario. Tax services will cost more; figure $1500 to $2000 a year for S-Corp tax paperwork. Make sure you engage a Certified Public Accountant (CPA) for all of your taxes. These services and expenses will be well worth it if you are actually making the type of income that would prompt you to choose to take the S-Corp election.

Payroll

You would have payroll in your business under two scenarios. The first is that you are making a substantial amount of income, in which case it makes sense to begin paying yourself a salary, along with distributing profits, rather than just taking simple distributions. The second is that you are ready to hire additional employees. Chapter 11 will discuss employees in more detail; for now, the simple rule is that if you want freedom, independence, and wealth, don't hire employees. Once you have attained a high level of success and income, you can revisit the idea of employing others under certain circumstances. Until then, make your business and coding practice a solo practice.

▓ **Rule**   As your primary goals are independence, wealth, and freedom, only add employees in rare cases (see Chapter 11 for more detail). You can attain all three of these goals through a solo practice, and generally don't need the extra weight of employees.

When deciding whether to pay yourself from your business, you need to consider income level, business structure, and tax consequences. The following scenarios will help you conceptualize the options you have regarding payroll based on these considerations:

1. **You are making $240,000 or less a year.** At this rate, you are making what someone in your position would be making in a year if they were employed by someone else, so keep your business as a simple LLC and do not use payroll. Do not hire employees; use only subcontractors. $240,000 should be a temporary stop on your path to wealth and independence.

2. **You are making $390,000 a year.** As discussed previously, in 2014, the highest "reasonable" income for an employed coder is around $240,000 a year, so you are making $150,000 more in profits than someone who is employed. The 2.9% tax rate on the $150,000 surplus is an annual cost of $4,350 more in Medicare tax that you have to pay as an LLC rather than an S-Corp. However, there are costs associated with having someone prepare your S-Corp taxes (approx. $2,000 a year) and administer payroll ($250 to $1,000 a year). Additionally, by the time you deduct business expenses and similar items from your taxes, you likely won't make the full $150,000 in profit. At $390,000, you are most likely not earning enough to make the swap to S-Corp profitable solely for the tax savings. You also aren't making enough to hire employees. $390,000 is really the minimum annual target amount you should be making as an independent coder, and you should continue to keep things as simple as possible at this level, which means having no employees (but you can have as many subcontractors as you want).

3. **You are making more than $500,000 a year.** At this
level, you can seriously consider the S-Corp election for
your LLC. Your profit is high enough that the 2.9% savings in Medicare taxes you will get will be greater than
the costs associated with administrating this S-Corp.
In this case, you could pay yourself a yearly salary of
$240,000 as a "reasonable" salary, to comply with IRS
regulations. Everything over the $240,000 is profit. If you
have $260,000 profit, eliminating the 2.9% Medicare tax
is an annual savings of $7,540, which means after you pay
for payroll and additional tax preparation, you can walk
away with a few extra grand in your pocket.

Rule Ultimately, you have to decide when the additional headache of payroll and S-Corp taxes
is worth your time and worth the additional savings. $500,000 is really the minimum income you'll
want to be making before you even consider the election for S-Corp. Know that making the election
is extremely simple (it just requires filing a tax form, best done by an attorney or tax consultant to
make sure it is right), but there is no going back to a simple LLC with the same company once you
have done this.

Insurance

Your goals are to become independent and wealthy through your business,
and to do this you must be able to engage with as many different kinds
of companies and people as you can without hindrance or concern. With
incorporation as an LLC or an S-Corp, you have the protections needed for
financial aspects of your business; however, you have nothing to secure you
from lawsuits or secure you if you suffer a personal injury. You must obtain
personal and professional insurance coverage.

Professional Insurance

Although it is not a legal requirement, you really should always carry professional insurance. The cost is based on your income level and the coverage
provided (it will become more expensive as you earn more income), and generally is very affordable. Some insurance companies have specialized packages
for businesses that specialize in technology and software delivery. Talk with
an insurance agent to determine what packages are available. You should be
able to get a policy that covers you up to a few million dollars for any liability
related to coding. If you are making $300,000 or less, this policy costs a few
hundred dollars. If you are making more, the cost increases, naturally, but it is
a very minor expense relative to your income.

In many cases, you will not be able to engage on a project without proof of basic insurance coverage (usually $1 million or $2 million minimum). Most companies that you can subcontract through require their subcontractors to carry insurance limits that match their own. Many industries also have specific insurance requirements for contractors; for instance, if you are working in the health care industry and have access to any personal medical information (such as would be the case if you are doing database-related work for any type of health care company), then you must have coverage. Various governmental mandates require coverage for businesses (coverage for potential Health Insurance Portability and Accountability [HIPAA] violations are an excellent example), and if you want to work on projects in these industries, you must have proof of insurance.

A policy may offer several options in the riders and additional coverages that you can sign up for, many of which are completely irrelevant to you (the terrorism protection option, for example), but the basic coverages that you need are shown in Figure 5-1. The limits that you need may change with time, but the insurance provider will offer you only standard tiers from which to choose, and it is just a matter of selecting coverage that either matches the requirements of a company you are doing business with or aligns with the type of project work you are doing. Figure 5-1 shows a scanned copy of an actual Technology Package Policy, showing the professional coverage along with the premium amounts (which are the actual costs to you).

COVERAGE PART		PREMIUM
Commercial Liability		$550.00
Each Occurrence Limit	$1,000,000	
Personal & Advertising Injury Limit (Any One Person/Organization)	$1,000,000	
Medical Expense Limit (Any One Person)	$10,000	
Damages To Premises Rented To You (Any One Premises)	$300,000	
Products/Completed Operations Aggregate Limit	Included	
General Aggregate Limit	$2,000,000	
Commercial Property		$550.00
Total Property Limit	$75,000	
Largest Property Risk	$75,000	
Technology Professional Liability Errors And Omissions		$6,616.00
Each Claim Limit	$3,000,000	
Annual Aggregate Limit	$3,000,000	
Deductible	$0	
Retroactive Date	02/01/2009	

Figure 5-1. Example of professional insurance coverage, including premiums

Personal Insurance

There are three types of personal insurance that you should incorporate into your structure: health, life, and disability. Although you don't purchase these policies directly through your business, they do protect you and your assets against various events. You can certainly shop for each of these policies on your own, but you will reduce your time if you work with an agent, ideally one whom you can work with online and over the phone.

Signing up for each of these policies takes time, even after you have decided which is most appropriate for you. Save yourself some of this time by having an agent do much of the work for you. In most cases, you'll be able to do everything from your office or home. For example, the application process for each of these policies typically requires blood work to be done, and the insurance agent will coordinate a time at which a technician can meet you at your home or office to draw your blood.

Rule Try to find an agent who can work with you to get coverage on all three types of insurance. There are many agents who work across industries, and who can present to you options that cover all types. Working with a single agent can save you time in what is a very time-consuming process.

Some thoughts on each of the types of insurance are given here:

1. **Health insurance**. Expensive and generally less comprehensive than you would hope, health insurance is nonetheless a requirement. As a person who is working toward wealth and independence, you should plan to take care of all of your healthcare costs out of pocket, except in the event of catastrophe. Try and find a high-deductible policy that has 100% coverage after the deductible is met. You don't need the coverage that the media and the politicians advertise, which includes all of the nickel-and-dime costs for incidental costs. You simply need coverage for major things that could cost tens of thousands of dollars (surgery, emergencies, etc.).

Rule Many people have sold themselves for company benefits. That is, many people are reluctant to leave an employer because of the health coverage that is provided. As an independent businessperson, you need to think very differently. Pay for a policy that covers emergencies, pay for the rest out of pocket, and work to keep yourself healthy (see Chapter 13).

---

2.   **Life insurance.** Unfortunately, you will die at some point in the future. If you make it to old age, congratulations. If you don't, then you should have some other consolation. A life insurance policy is a great way to protect your family in the event that you don't make it to the winter of your life. There are endless options to life insurance, but if you don't like to throw your money away on something you don't believe will ever be used, try looking at Return of Premium policies. These are policies that will return all of the money you paid for them when the policy expires, assuming you are still alive. Over the course of 20 years, for a $2 million policy, that will be somewhere around $250,000. Regardless of what you choose, get a policy. As you gain wealth, you will most likely acquire property and incur debts, and you should have coverage for your family.

3.   **Disability insurance.** As a coder, the likelihood that you will become disabled to an extent that you can no longer work is very small, but it is still a possibility. Look at getting basic disability coverage. In some cases, there is disability built into your professional insurance package, but it never hurts to have additional coverage. Again, you can potentially find a Return of Premium policy that will ensure that you aren't just adding another expense for coverage that won't be used.

■ **Rule**   You can get by without personal and professional insurance, but if your goal is wealth and independence, then you should embrace these services and approach their purchase with an appreciation that you have the income to afford them. When you are young and have little income, this type of expense is something you would never consider. But as you acquire assets and/or your family size increases, you should buy policies that will protect you and those who depend on you.

Infrastructure

Your business should be extremely efficient in every aspect, from delivery and communications to infrastructure and incorporation. You want a minimalist environment, and one that is highly portable (so that you can do business from anywhere). You also want an environment that has a highly professional polish to it. Consider the following when building the infrastructure of your business:

1. **Office staff**. See Chapter 11 for more specific details, but the general message is simple: do not hire office staff. If you do hire employees, they should be billable resources, not office or support staff. You need to be your own secretary, as your business is dependent on access to you. Hire service providers for payroll, taxes, and other similar functions, but do not hire part-time or full-time staff that is dependent on you. Focus on your freedom and your independence, and use your wealth externally for the betterment of your world rather than for nonbillable internal staff.

2. **Accounting**. You need to be able to track your income and expenses and send invoices. You personally need to be able to administer your company, and should be doing all of the bookkeeping yourself (except payroll, if applicable). Use online software such as QuickBooks. The annual yearly fee is in the neighborhood of $400.

CASE STUDY

I have seen several businesses virtually destroyed by poor accounting and mistakes in bookkeeping. In all of these cases, the accounting was done by hired (and salaried) staff. As an independent businessperson and coder engaging on projects, your accounting is going to be extremely simple (even with employees), and you should plan to do all of the accounting yourself. In a few hours a month, you can send your invoices, track your expenses, issue profit distributions to yourself, and see the overall health of your company. If you hire someone to do your payroll, have them issue your paychecks (an entry in QuickBooks with all of the appropriate taxes taken out), but otherwise plan to do everything yourself.

---

3. **Business lines of credit**. Your bank has options for lines of credit. You should always have a line of credit available to you, and you should work with your bank to ensure you have the highest possible line offered. Try and get an unsecured line of credit. Some of the big chain banks have unsecured lines up to $100,000 available to high-income earners. Smaller banks require collateral. Find an option that gives you the flexibility to spend on high-expense, short-term costs that have low yearly fees. You need to be able to take every opportunity when it comes, and ensure that you are paying your vendors and subcontractors on time. Sometimes that means you need to take a temporary loan. You also need to be able to invest in yourself and your business, and you should have the tools necessary to be able to do this.

4. **Public-facing materials**. You want your externally facing public material to be solid and highly polished. This includes your website (more detail on this in Chapter 6), but also covers mundane materials such as envelopes, checks, and even the antiquated business card. You need to make sure all of these are of the highest quality, showing that you are willing to invest money in your own business. Your goal is to make those you do business with very comfortable doing business with you, particularly because you generally will be in an offsite setting. Your public-facing materials are what people see, and need to be very high end.

5. **Sending documents**. When you are sending anything of importance (copies of your books, letters of inquiry, follow-up materials from a sales call, etc.), send it via FedEx. Send it overnight. Spend the money to send it using the best options available.

6. **Mailing address**. For purposes of receiving mail or providing others with an address at which you do business, use a post office box. Generally speaking, you want to maintain ambiguity as to where your physical residence is. If you are working out of your home office, you don't want to share your home address with all of your clients. If you are working out of office space, you want to be able to

easily move around without having to constantly update your mailing address. Providing a post office box creates a separation between you and your business, and ensures no one can use Google Maps to locate where you work. It also allows you to pick up and go…and work from the beach for a month; just set up executive forwarding on your post office box, and get your mail wherever you are at.

Retirement Planning

There are many ideas about retirement planning, and everyone has a different approach. You will be making a large income, and certainly can set aside plenty of your resources for the future. When you are making a small income, putting aside a little early on in your career to ensure you can capitalize on compound interest over the course of a lifetime may be important. But when you are independent and wealthy, you have the freedom to rethink retirement and set aside funds in any way you choose.

You can certainly go the traditional route of IRAs and similar investment strategies, or you can take advantage of your situation and invest in things that interest you, aid others, or make life more enjoyable. Putting large sums of money away in your 30s so that you can live comfortably in your 70s is, in the common thoughts of economists and planners, a wise investment. But creating a life that will generate more freedom and wealth for yourself and others around you in the present is also an excellent way to plan for the future.

If you are generous, manage your funds wisely, and have a healthy view of the proper use of money, then you do not need to follow the traditional, well-advertised paths to saving for retirement. Be creative, invest in what you enjoy, use your resources to better the world, and trust that your generosity will be rewarded in the long run, regardless of your beliefs about the power of a 401k. The apostle James writes, "Come now, you who say, 'Today or tomorrow we will go to such and such a city, and spend a year there and engage in business and make a profit.' Yet you do not know what your life will be like tomorrow. You are just a vapor that appears for a little while and then vanishes away." Plan for the future, but realize that you live now and need to use your resources responsibly for the present; everything is temporary, and tomorrow may not come.

Conclusion

The setup and incorporation of your business should be rapid, and is entirely within your control. A name, an entity, and a bank account are all you need to begin working independently and making an income. You need to be aware of topics pertaining to payroll and taxes, and know everything about the administration of your business. Hiring professionals to assist you in time-consuming activities such as the creation of paychecks and preparation of your corporate taxes is an intelligent use of funds, whereas hiring employees (especially nonbillable ones) should be avoided. Keep focused on your ultimate goals of wealth and independence, and ensure that your business structure supports these.

■ **Rule**   If setting up your business entity and getting the banking requirements and paperwork in order take you weeks or months, then you need to seriously consider whether you are ready for the path of business independence. The ability to execute quickly on known tasks is critical to your success.

Advertising and Marketing

The Science of Lead Creation

No one lights a lamp and puts it in a place where it will be hidden, or under a bowl. Instead, they put it on its stand, so that those who come in may see the light.

—Luke 11:33

Untapped business opportunities exist all around you. Regardless of the economy, the region, or the market, opportunities for work, growth, and the generation of wealth are plentiful. There are a lot of projects and a lot of money out there to be had. Your challenge is to figure out how to find and acquire both. You are working in an abundant framework, in which the resources that you are after are virtually endless. You only have to figure out how to capture a miniscule fraction of what is available. In this chapter, you'll discover how to use marketing and advertising to ensure that clients can find you, and that your value is broadcast to the world.

▨ **Rule** In the most difficult of times, entrepreneurial people figure out how to find business and grow rich. In the most prosperous of times, there are people who can't make it, who end up broke, jobless, and on the streets. The technology industry to date has had some well-publicized bumps, and some leaner years, but throughout there have been tremendous opportunities. There is more work out there than there are resources to do the work.

As a solo service provider, your approach to advertising and marketing is considerably different from that of a larger company. Your primary focus is to publish technical literature. Writing a book as an employee of a company is a labor of love, and one that enables you to claim that you have published something, but it does not have any real impact on your income, your career, or your ability to build your employer's business. As an independent coder, on the other hand, nothing has a greater impact on your business than to publish a book or article commercially. Doing so creates leads, builds your network, and enables you to sell your services to a very wide audience that you would not have access to otherwise.

Your secondary focus is to present a highly polished image to the business world. As a technical provider, your web presence is the most visible reflection of your technical savvy, as all of your clients and contacts interact with you on the Internet. If you take your business seriously, the majority of your work will be remote, and you will need to make sure people have a way to know you without having to meet you in person. You must invest in your virtual image and periodically revise it. A dull and static website that you created in a few hours does not show that you are technically sophisticated, so you need to work with a marketing firm to create the level of presentation that is appropriate.

This chapter describes how to publish and how to present yourself. These two areas of concentration are the only activities within the realm of advertising and marketing that you need to pursue to create leads that will turn into business opportunities and billable engagements. Diligent and ongoing attention to advertising and marketing throughout the course of your independent career creates a force that supports the continuous growth of your business and the achievement of your goals of independence and wealth.

■ **Rule** As a solo practitioner, you are a marketer, an advertiser, and a salesperson, but do not plan to do these alone. Work with skilled, professional individuals or firms that specialize in the various aspects of advertising and marketing you engage in. Your budget should be high, and your expectations should be higher.

Publishing

Publishing technical books and articles is the only advertising activity you need to engage in as an independent coder. Your ability to find work depends on two key things: your capacity to get in front of the buyer (the person at the client that has the actual economic purchasing power for your services), and your success in establishing trust with the buyer that you are an expert at what you do, and the most appropriate resource to work with. Publishing books and articles accomplishes both of these aims, and sets you on a career trajectory that will be virtually unstoppable.

▧ **Rule** Commercially published books are of incredible value to your business, while self-published print or electronic books are not. The former open doors and create connections, while the latter simply supplement aspects of your work.

Although writing can be difficult and time-consuming, the dividends that it can pay are enormous. If you publish commercially, new opportunities will open up and potential clients will seek to hire you for project work based on what you have written. You may be asked to speak on topics you've written on, which further expands your audience for potential new business. You'll expand your network and improve relationships with existing clients and contacts. You will be perceived as an expert, and will have a much easier time convincing prospects that your skills are as advertised. In short, if done strategically, publishing commercially creates an advertising engine that generates leads that are ready to engage your services. You won't have to proactively sell your services; instead, you will simply have to choose the best opportunities from among the many that are offered to you.

If you publish intelligently, your business will be transformed. If you write with the intention that your publication will create unexpected opportunities, it will enable you to move to a new level in your business. If, on the other hand, you labor through the writing of the book and put no thought or intention into the work other than to "publish a book," your book will quickly fade and have virtually no positive impact on your business. Your intent as you write has a far greater impact on the final manuscript than you can imagine. Your energy will come across in the words you write and the concepts you illustrate, and leave the reader either impressed or weary. Robert Frost wrote, "No tears in the writer, no tears in the reader. No surprise in the writer, no surprise in the reader." Be enthusiastic throughout the process, and your creation will cause opportunities to materialize.

▧ **Rule** Publishing a book is a major undertaking, but it is also the single most effective tool in new business generation for the solo practitioner. If your advertising activities consist of nothing other than consistently publishing new material, you will have done all of the advertising you need to do to have a highly successful practice.

CASE STUDY

When I started my business, I wanted to see what value publishing a well-thought-out and targeted book would have for my workload. Although I had co-authored one book previously, I had not written with any intent to build a business, and, consequently, it was not a book that I could use directly to grow my practice. With the goal of writing a book that would be a platform for my growth and success, I put together a proposal, sent it to the publisher, and was surprised days later to have a contract.

The book was about a specific application of a platform that I had extensive experience with, and my intention behind the publication of the book was to find a high-paying customer and expand my business. Within two weeks after publication, I received a phone call from a company asking if I was available to work with them on setting up their environment for this platform. This led to a project worth $150,000, and was the first of several projects that stemmed directly from the publication of this book.

Today, I can trace a sizeable percentage of my work to the network that has grown from my technical publications.

Ten Steps to Publishing a Book

The following steps give an overview of what you need to do to publish a technical book. Your path to writing is wide open; you just have to know the steps and be confident in your subject matter.

■ **Rule**   The publishing industry is constantly looking for good authors to write on appropriate subjects. If you have current technical skills and can write well, the door is open for you to write a commercial book.

Step 1: Select Several Topics

Identify several technical topics that you can write about that are unique and for which you can deliver valuable content. For your first book, think of topics that you have ample material for, and that have been central to a large number of projects you have delivered. Ideally, choose topics that are relevant to project work you are actively doing, as you'll be able to piggyback on some of the code that you are writing and conversations that you are having.

Step 2: Create the Title and Summary

For each of the ideas you have, create a working title and write a paragraph describing what the proposed book would be about. You should be able to brainstorm and write several ideas within a very short time. Don't labor through this activity. It should come naturally and easily, as it must be something that you have extensive experience with. If it isn't easy, throw the idea out, as you'll never be able to write hundreds of pages on a topic if you can't write a paragraph about it.

Step 3: Contact a Publisher

Once you have summarized your ideas in writing, reach out to a technical book publisher by sending an e-mail to the editorial board. You can usually find all of the information you need online in order to contact a publisher and the board; additionally, you can find contact information in the opening pages of most technical books. Introduce yourself, give a short summary of your background, and list the titles and summaries you came up with. Ask if the publisher is interested in publishing a book about any of the topics.

Step 4: Submit Your Proposal

If the editorial board (or a specific editor) is directly interested in one or more of your topics, they will ask you to put together a much more detailed proposal of what you plan to write, along with details about the chapters, the audience, and the market. If the publisher is not interested in any of the ideas you have submitted, respond by asking which topics they are currently interested in. The editor you are corresponding with will have a list of topics he or she is looking for authors to write about, and will gladly share some of the working concepts with you. If you have marketable coding skills, there likely will be something in the list that you'll be able to write about.

Step 5: Finalize Your Proposal

You will have several rounds with the editor to refine your proposal into a final version that is agreeable to both you and the publisher. The proposal serves two primary purposes. First, it ensures that you have thought through the full book, can write coherently, and can produce a deliverable. Second, it ensures that you have a product that is saleable. The initial sale is to the publisher's editorial board, while the next sale is to the public.

■ **Rule**   A book usually takes between six and nine months to publish after you get approval on your proposal.

Step 6: Receive a Contract

Once your proposal is accepted, the publisher will offer you a contract. Typically, the contract states that you will deliver the first three chapters by a certain date, and the full manuscript by a specific later date. It also sets forth your royalty and advance payment plan (if applicable).

■ **Rule** Your goal in writing a book is not to get paid royalties (though you will receive some compensation). Very few technical books have a broad enough audience that the royalties are of any significance. Do not concern yourself with the royalty breakdown, or what you might get paid (often, these terms are not even negotiable). Concern yourself primarily with the delivery dates, and know that your revenue will come via other channels opened by the publication of the book.

Step 7: Write

There are many approaches to writing, but the simple rule here is to produce content. You are not writing a novel, and no one is looking for exceptional prose. Your intent should be to deliver top-quality information that isn't easily available elsewhere, with code samples, screenshots, and other applicable information targeted to the technical audience you are writing for. You want to produce unique, original content that you can put together from projects and code samples you are very familiar with, and that covers concepts you have a high level of expertise with. You don't want to waste time writing material that is new to you, or for which you have to do significant research. Focus on speed and quality, and leverage code, exercises, and illustrations heavily. Think about what you want to find when you are searching for how to do something—you want actual examples, and often skip the sections of prose and explanatory detail.

■ **Rule** Treat your book as a high-priority billable project. It has a greater long-term significance to you than any single project you are working on at the moment, and although it will not pay immediate dividends, the impact it can have on your long-term business is of such high value that you should consider it the top priority.

Step 8: Respond to Edits

During the writing process, editors, copyeditors, and technical reviewers will review your work, make revisions, and ask you questions. In turn, you must review the revisions and accept or reject them, and respond to the questions. You need to allot time for this review cycle, as it is a requirement of delivery. Try to minimize the amount of time you spend on this portion of the process by trusting others to assist here, but ultimately this material is yours and should carry your voice and your approach. You generally have a lot of control over what revisions are made to your content, but it does take some time to work through this editing cycle.

Step 9: Compile "Front Matter" Material

After you have written the main content of your book, you will be asked to put together the material that might be inconsequential to the purely technical reader, but is of high value to you and higher level business readers. This material, known as "front matter" because it appears at the beginning of the book, includes nontechnical sections such as your biography, a foreword, and your introduction to the book. Each of these elements is very important, and you should approach them thoughtfully. These are the key sections that allow you to speak directly to your readers and to potential clients.

Biography

This is your opportunity to summarize all of your skills and introduce yourself to readers; think of it as a mini-résumé. The biography typically is included on the book's product page on Amazon.com and other online booksellers, so it will often be located by anyone who searches for your name online. This section is also often the first thing that a reader will turn to. Make this a public-facing overview of who you are and what you do, and make sure to list options for contacting you. Include your e-mail address and website URL in your biography, and invite readers to contact you.

Introduction

If you are writing heavy technical content, it is very unlikely that anyone is going to read every word of your book. A coder will turn to a specific section of interest, but isn't likely to read the book as a whole. A businessperson won't read any of the technical content, but will likely peruse the foreword and the introduction, along with your biography. The introduction should be very business focused, and outline the value of the technology you are writing about to the business user. Consider this your opportunity to promote the value of the platform or technology you are writing about, so that someone contemplating using the platform in their environment will be sold on its use before they ever speak with you.

Foreword

This has the potential to be the most valuable section in your book. The foreword is written by another person who has experience or expertise in the subject your book addresses. This means you can reach out to virtually anyone who has any affiliation with what you are writing about and ask them to take part in your book. This has value to the person writing the foreword because they get their name and credentials on the cover. It has value to you because you get to initiate a conversation with someone you want to open up a channel of communication with. Think of the foreword as a business opportunity for both you and the person writing the foreword. In some cases, having someone write a foreword to your book creates a relationship that opens up billable project opportunities for both of you, either with each other or with others.

Rule Invite to participate in your book people that you want to extend an existing relationship or open a new relationship with. The publisher typically allows you to choose the technical reviewer and the author of the foreword, and you should take this as an opportunity to choose people who can open new avenues of business for you (and vice versa).

Step 10: Prepare to Reach Out

After you complete all of the content and front matter, your book is on track to publish. While you are waiting for this to occur (which usually takes an additional month), think of ways to use your book to build your business and increase your network. See the upcoming section "Utilizing Your Published Material" for ideas about how to use your book to generate business, acquire clients, and close sales.

Rule Be prepared for criticism. The moment you create something and put it out there for public consumption, critics and fools will descend. No matter the quality of your work, or the value it contains for the market you are targeting, someone will give you a one-star review on Amazon.com and question your intelligence and integrity. You have to take this criticism in stride. Know that many people feel compelled to be ugly and negative, and it is a rare person who engages with the world with words that build rather than destroy.

Publishing an Article

Publishing an article is surprisingly labor intensive, and the revision and editorial process is often more involved than for an entire book. An article carries less weight than a book, but the moment it publishes it is immediately seen by a much wider audience. An article has a very short shelf life (generally just the month that it publishes), so its value in ongoing advertising is limited (it can't be utilized in the same way that a book can be). But, it can generate leads, drive people and business to you, and it certainly gives additional credence to your skillset and enhances your résumé.

Rule   Try to publish an article at the same time you are publishing a book. The article can be a unique aspect of something you are writing about in the book, covering a specific concept in more detail or expanding a discussion about something you are presenting. By working to leverage content that overlaps, your article will help publicize your book, and the value of each will be enhanced by the other.

The steps to publish an article are similar to those previously outlined for a book, but differ in intensity and time. You will spend less time writing the initial content and far more time editing. In many cases, you will be asked to rewrite entire sections of your article to align with the requirements of the editor you are working with. Generally, an article will publish three to six months after the time you get your contract from the magazine publisher.

CASE STUDY

The first article I published was with *MSDN Magazine*. It took almost as much work to write a six-page article as it did to write an entire book. After months of rewriting the content to match the editor's requirements, the article was finally published. Within a day of publication, a company contacted me saying the article covered the exact type of solution they were working to implement. The discussion led to a six-figure project and a long-term business relationship.

Utilizing Your Published Material

After you have published a book or an article, you have an incredible piece of advertising that you can use to initiate conversations, reach out to potential customers, and solidify your foothold with existing clients. A publication will certainly get your name out in front of a target audience of readers and lead to unexpected leads and conversations without your having to do anything, but its greatest value is in how you personally use it to advertise and build your business. The following list outlines ways in which to maximize the advertising and marketing value of your publication.

Rule The publisher will give you several free copies when you write a book, but you will want to purchase many more to use for advertising and marketing. Generally, publishers offer deep discounts on author copies. Take whatever royalty or advance you might earn and spend it all on additional copies. Set aside additional budget to buy more copies as needed. This is the best use of any advertising dollars you will spend.

Offer It to Known Contacts

Send e-mail to colleagues and clients (especially former ones who you are not actively working with) who may be interested in the content of your book or article (or who you have not spoken with in a long time), and let them know you have published a new book or article. In the case of a book, offer to send a free copy.

In the case of an article, send a link to the online version or offer to send a free copy of the magazine it was published in. You are offering something of value, and something you worked hard to create. At a minimum, it enables you to reestablish communication with people and offer them something they might benefit from. In many cases, they will respond and a conversation will start, which can lead to project opportunities or chances to build and extend your network.

Rule When sending copies of your book or article, use FedEx or similar overnight service. You want to make sure that the book or magazine reaches the recipient directly, and is not overlooked. You've invested a lot of time and effort writing the book, and this is your opportunity to use it to improve your network and generate leads and opportunities. Spend the money to package and deliver it professionally.

CASE STUDY

Don't limit potential recipients only to people who you think would be interested in the specific material covered in your published work. People like to be thought of, and the offer of receiving a free book in the mail is almost always taken. In one case, after I had published a short book on a specific application of a technology, I reached out to a client I had not done business with in over two years. I let my contact there know I had published a book, and asked if he would like a copy. He said he would, but more importantly he said he had some project work available, and was glad that I had contacted him. We discussed the project briefly over e-mail, which led to a six-month, $6,000-a-month contract.

Use It to Solidify Introductions

When talking with potential clients who have contacted you directly, or who have been referred to you by partner companies in your network, you are often asked to introduce yourself. During your introduction, be brief, mention your skills, and always let them know you have authored a book or article that may be of interest to them. Offer to send a free copy. This establishes you immediately as an expert and changes the tone of the conversation. It also gives you a concrete and effective way to follow up with the potential client. A book with your name on it arriving at their office in a day or two is an excellent way to set yourself apart in their mind as they are determining what resources to use to staff their project. Everything else being equal, the person with the published book will get the job.

Use It to Open Conversations with New Contacts

Identify individuals and organizations that you would like to do business with, and reach out to them by offering to send a free copy of your published work to them. You can contact them via e-mail or phone. This is the closest activity to "cold calling" that you will ever need to participate in as an independent coder. This enables you to open doors and start conversations that you otherwise could not have. Having something of value to offer potential contacts makes the cold call easy for you and much more palatable to them. Write a cover letter, package it with additional materials that you may have (see the section "Additional Collateral" later in this chapter), and send the package by overnight delivery. In the cover letter, introduce yourself, your qualifications, and the value that you can bring through your services. Let the contact know that you would like to meet with them by phone or in person at their convenience and at your cost. Don't try to sell anything, and clearly state you are just interested in discussing whether you may be able to assist them in some way.

Use It to Sell Your Services

During a conversation that may lead to a sale, make sure to offer free copies of your published material to the client. When someone is deciding whether to work with you, or whether to commit to purchasing your services, the offer of a book with your name on it can close the deal.

Your Web Presence

If you publish a book or article, you must have a professional and highly polished online presence to support that publication. If you have not yet published anything, your online presence must be even more polished. Hire experts to build your website. Invest the time and money to ensure that you have the most professional web presence possible. Hire a professional photographer to take your photo. This website is your public face, and is often the deciding factor as to whether or not someone will do business with you.

It is easy for a technologist to create a basic information website. A few minutes on Word Press will get you a basic template with which you can create a website. However, a website built from a template is essentially an expanded business card, and won't give you the polished look that you need for your website. The goal of your website is to solidify your expertise and value in the mind of viewers. These viewers are potential or existing clients. A basic website or blog is not an appropriate vehicle to communicate your expertise or offerings. Hire a professional to help you create the messaging for your website. Work with a firm that specializes not only in developing your image and voice on your site, but in creating your overall web presence.

Your web presence is more than your website. Nothing but professional activities should appear when someone searches for your name. Personal interests and postings (such as Facebook) can only be detrimental when prospective clients are researching you, while a complete lack of web presence will make you look like an amateur. As an independent businessperson who depends on the Internet for your business and success, you want to do everything you can to ensure that the Web is a place for business life, not for personal life.

■ **Rule** Invest in professional photos and integrate them into your online presence. In most cases, you will be a remote resource on projects you engage on, and your website may be the only place where people you work with have an opportunity to see you. Establishing rapport with a client is often easier if they can put a face with your name.

Work with a marketing firm. Do your research to find the best people in the business, and plan to pay top dollar for the best firm. As your business income grows, so should your investment in your online presence.

CASE STUDY

I wanted to expand my work into a particular industry and engage with multiple resources, but I didn't have any immediate way to do so. I had delivered services within this industry many times over the years, and knew I had the skills to do this successfully, but my contacts were limited for building out a larger project. Deciding to put some energy toward this, I contacted a marketing firm and asked them to put together a plan for updating my website and creating some basic marketing collateral that I could use.

The firm gave me a plan and a price, and we moved forward. They revised my website and created high-quality brochures and several cover letters, completing their work within 45 days. Two weeks later, completely unrelated to anything specific that I did with this marketing exercise, a client contacted me and requested five full-time resources to engage on a project within the industry I had targeted. This was the largest single request for services I had ever received, and it led to significant revenue for an extended period of time.

If I had not engaged in the marketing exercise, I do not believe this client would have come along. Though the client contacted me for reasons completely unrelated to the marketing campaign, the result was the same. My goal of finding a large, multi-resource project within this industry was attained within weeks of having completed the new marketing project. Often, the energy we put into our marketing efforts leads us to the goals and objectives we are after, whether or not anyone ever sees the updated website, the brochures, or any other component specific to the marketing work. It is the thought and intention that makes the difference.

Throughout this book I stress the idea that positive thinking is responsible for much of your success. The concept that the power of thought has a direct impact on the physical world around us is as old as the human experience. In the Buddhist text called the Dhammapada, it is written, "All that we are is the result of what we have thought: it is founded on our thoughts, it is made up of our thoughts." Even in more mundane activities such as the marketing of your services, your thoughts and intentions will drive the success or failure of the actions you take.

Additional Collateral

A marketing firm will often recommend collateral material that supplements your web presence and your publications. Additionally, you may come up with some material on your own, or in tandem with other professionals. Some of the additional items you may want to include in your marketing portfolio are outlined in the following list. Consider all of these to be of secondary importance, and items that have value only in conjunction with your publishing and web presence. These items can heighten your air of professionalism and polished look, but none of them alone or in combination will lead directly to additional work.

1. **Marketing materials**. When you work with a marketing firm to develop your website, you will have the option to get additional materials such as electronic letterhead, brochures, logos, and similar items. In the technical field, these have very little value to you, but you may have reason to use them in two cases. The first case relates to the letterhead. When you are hiring an employee or going through the process of establishing a line of credit, you may be asked to verify that you are the business owner. In these cases, the verification process with the bank or with the employee's creditors (such as rental agencies) almost always requires that you provide a signed letter that includes your letterhead. The second case relates to the brochure. If you are sending a free book to a potential client that you have not done business with before, you may want to include a brochure with the book. A brochure that outlines your value proposition and your skills can occasionally be a better introduction than a résumé.

2. **Self-published print, electronic, and audio books**. If you are a specialist within a specific area of technology, and you have something unique to share, you may want to put together a small publication that you can distribute via your website. In general, the effort required to create a self-published title is better applied toward generating a commercially published book or article. It is highly unlikely that you will ever land a client through one of these self-published forms of media, and the level of effort to create them is significantly higher than the value you will get from them as supplemental material for your online presence.

3. **Business cards**. These are immensely outdated, but people still carry them. When someone hands you their business card, it is great to be able to respond by giving one of your own. You may also want to include one when you are sending out free copies of your book or article.

4. **Social media**. For someone involved in higher-level business strategy or more consumer-oriented topics, social media may valuable, but for the technologist who is focused on coding and delivery, the only social media that may be of some real value is LinkedIn. Twittering about your C# components will lead nowhere, but having your basic résumé in place on LinkedIn will ensure that you are part of the professional online network. Make sure you keep your information relatively current on LinkedIn, but don't look to it as a way for you to find work or expand your network.

5. **Blogging**. Many coders write technical blogs. Blogging on technical topics is virtually worthless to you as a marketing mechanism or as a lead-generation device. Blogging does have two benefits. First, it gives you a place to document something you may want to archive for later reference (for example, you figured out how to configure IIS security for a specific WCF implementation, and you need to record it for yourself). Second, it gives other developers a good resource to reference. This is a friendly gesture, but it won't lead to business. If you are an employee, it is a great use of time, but if you are an independent developer and in business for yourself, a technical blog focused on code and platform configurations is of questionable value.

Rule Blogging and social media have virtually no value to the technologist, but they do have value to the more business-focused entrepreneur. If your career path leads you from a highly successful independent coder to a highly successful businessperson focusing on issues not directly related to code and platforms, you can reassess the value of social media and blogging.

A Word on Branding

A common notion is that you need to create a brand for yourself to maximize your marketing and advertising impact. There are a few things to mention about branding, but the key takeaway is that you do not need a distinctive brand for yourself or your business to achieve high levels of success. Your skill and your professionalism will set you apart and open doors to many opportunities that others with lesser abilities will not have. A strong work ethic, top-level skills, and the ability to find, sell, and deliver on work do not constitute an official brand or something that uniquely defines you, but they almost always guarantee that you will have a steady stream of high-income projects.

The chance that someone in the business of selling their services can successfully develop brand recognition is extremely low, regardless of the amount of marketing effort or dollars they expend. This is because, in services, branding comes with time, experience, and success. You can certainly participate in activities that will strengthen your name recognition, but your goal is not fame. Your goals are independence and wealth, and you can achieve these without brand recognition.

If you end up in a position where your name is well known or you can create a brand, pursue it. By the time you have a marketable name or brand, you will have already achieved your initial goals of success and wealth, and can move on to broader goals and higher ambitions, far beyond the scope of this book.

Conclusion

Your marketing and advertising activities are important to the growth and endurance of your business. If you do not participate in these activities, you will not achieve your potential, and your goals of true success, independence, and wealth will be elusive. Writing and publishing books and articles are long-term projects, and don't lead to immediate sales, but as soon as they are published, opportunities will materialize that you can easily turn into sales. Having a strong web presence may bring direct business to you, but the true value of it is to solidify your expertise, give people a face to associate with your work, and complement your publications. In all of your advertising and marketing actions, make sure you have a strong and positive intention, and that you define your expectations of your efforts before you begin; the thought that is behind your actions will ultimately drive the success or failure of any single activity or publication.

Sales

The Art of Networking, Prospecting, and Closing

Buying and selling is now regarded as something ordinary, like the art of reading and writing; everyone is now trained to it even when he is not a tradesman exercising himself daily in the art; precisely as formerly in the period of uncivilised humanity, everyone was a hunter and exercised himself day by day in the art of hunting.

—Friedrich Nietzsche, *The Gay Science*

All of us are familiar with the basics of buying and selling. Generally, we excel at the task of buying, and fear the task of selling. Though selling is "now regarded as something ordinary," it is a highly misunderstood concept. Although you must engage in selling to sustain your independent practice, you need to sell only in a limited capacity. You need to know the art of selling within the world in which you work, but you do not need to learn the strategies outlined in countless sales books, and you do not need to take sales courses. To sell your services successfully, you need to do solid work, put in place an advertising and marketing engine, build a strong and ever-growing network, know how to mine your network, and be able to close on leads.

As a coder seeking business success as a solo practitioner, you must know how to sell, but you do not need to be a salesperson. A salesperson is a pusher of goods or services and does not implement or take part in deliverables. You are an implementer of solutions who happens to be responsible for selling the work you engage on. Be good at what you do, and work will find you. Be good at what you do and be good at selling, and work will find you and you will find work. You must take part in creating opportunities and growing your practice, rather than being a passive receiver of what comes to you and simply keeps you employed.

Rule You do not have to sell anything to be able to engage on projects. Many independent contractors use an agent to place them on projects. These agents take a cut of the income and generally ensure that the developer has constant work and is staffed consistently from project to project. In this case, the contractor is taking no active role in sales, other than to be the commodity that the agent is selling. This is a viable way to land jobs, but it is not a path to wealth and independence, nor is it a way to operate at your highest ability. You do not want to be a common laborer with a time commodity sold by others; you want to be a creator of services who controls to some degree demand and market share.

Selling is an acquired skill. The more you practice it, the more proficient you become, and the more comfortable you are selling. There are three primary areas that you need to concentrate on to acquire this skill: growing and utilizing your network, finding new leads and opportunities at the appropriate time (called *prospecting*), and converting leads into sold projects from which you receive income. These three areas are the focus of the discussion in this chapter.

You should find that the techniques that you need to learn to sell the work you do come naturally to you. Portions of these techniques are an extension of what you are already doing within many of your projects; namely, identifying a need and determining scope. The additional technique in selling is that you must attach a price to every project and convince a buyer to give you money to implement it. Effectively executing on these techniques is integral to the growth and success of your business and to the attainment of your goals of wealth and independence.

Rule Actively engaging in sales transforms you from a coder who participates in one project at a time into a businessperson who has multiple simultaneous projects and constant future work in the pipeline. You do not need an agent or a placement firm, and you can control the flavor of the projects you accept and how, where, and when you work.

Networking

The success of your sales activity is based largely on your ability to build your network and communicate with people in this network. Your network contains all of your potential work-related opportunities. Working to maintain and grow this network through solid delivery, referrals, and your advertising and marketing work (outlined in Chapter 6) ensures that you constantly have a pool from which to draw paying business. You do not have to create a vast network, or invest a great amount of time in traditional networking activities. A very small network composed of strategic partners and repeat clients is sufficient to grow and sustain a high-powered and successful private practice.

You are in the services industry, and services are purchased by people. You may have a corporate focus on your implementations that are relevant only to a certain audience, and you may be able to talk technically about any aspect of a platform or an industry, but ultimately you are speaking to individuals who will determine whether or not they want to do business with you. Your ability to sell is based initially on getting in front of people, and ultimately on your ability to communicate and connect with people.

Never view your network solely as a way to find your next job. View it as a two-way lead-generation exchange. You must consistently bring leads and opportunities to people in your network if you expect to consistently receive leads and opportunities from this network. The more you invest in helping others improve their own businesses, the more they will invest in helping you build yours.

In all business interactions you have, always think of ways to include people in your network. By doing so, you will find that the conversation regarding what you can assist with is infinitely broader. If a client wants you to write a custom application but also has questions about a particular area you don't have direct exposure to, you can tell the client what you do know, and then offer to bring in one of your contacts that specializes in this area to discuss it with the client in more detail. Being able to bring additional resources to the table improves your value to your client and also to members in your network.

Build your network through every means you can think of, but always remember that you must bring something of value to others if you want something of value from others. You are not in business to take; you are in business to build, and that means building up everyone around you so that they may build you up. Creating new opportunities for people in your network is the quickest way to have a network of endless opportunities for you.

The Importance of Partnerships

Always be looking within your network for potential strategic partnerships (external to your business; not legal partners within your company structure). As an independent businessperson, your ability to align yourself with partners will determine the rate at which you grow and achieve higher levels of success. The most lucrative and long-lasting partnerships for an independent coder are those with consulting and staffing firms. These groups, whether large or small, are constantly looking for talent to staff their projects. They also often build solutions with the latest technology. Working with these firms in an ongoing manner will ensure that your skills remain current and that you have a steady flow of subcontract work. Depending on the flavor of the partnership, it can also result in both you and the partner assisting each other in creating bigger project opportunities.

■ **Rule** Aligning yourself with other firms is similar to working with a high-powered sales team. You can rely on their sales engine to create the opportunities that fuel their business, while you focus on the delivery work that comes out of these sales.

You never know who will be the link to your next opportunity or to a partnership with a firm. Among the many reasons you must treat everyone you encounter with respect, one is that they may be the link to your next project or contact. On many of your projects, you will be working with developers who have relationships with various staffing and consulting firms. If you do good work on a project and create a strong relationship with the people you are working with, it is possible that they will introduce you to contacts within their firm or agency.

In turn, if you come across someone who is pleasant to work with and has deep technical skills, you can refer them to people in your network.

CASE STUDY

After I had worked with a client for about 6 months, the client hired a full-time person to take over my work. The woman they hired had been independent for years, but was looking for long-term, permanent employment. She was sharp and worked extremely hard. The knowledge transfer went quickly, and during this transition time, she introduced me to a key contact at a large staffing and consulting firm. I spoke with the contact, and over the course of several months developed a working relationship and eventually engaged on a project through the firm. Over the course of several years, this professional relationship turned into a true business partnership, where we were both able to expand the types of offerings and increase the number of clients; the firm through its marketing and name recognition, and I through specific skills that I brought to the table. A partnership that now leads to a sizeable percentage of my annual revenue was established through a contact from a developer I was working with on a single project years earlier.

Most partnerships come from long-term relationships with consulting or staffing firms that you do delivery work for. If you are working purely as a billable resource and doing only project-related delivery work, you'll likely maintain a relationship with the firm that leads to project work on an ongoing basis. However, if you rise above delivery and try to expand the firm's relationships with clients that it places you with, you'll increase your value to the firm and begin to be seen as someone who can help build their business. If you bring in new clients and help the firm sell work, you will eventually be seen as a partner. As a partner, you will be able to help sell work, set fees, and determine how to engage, which is an excellent place to be as an independent party.

■ **Rule**   You cannot force partnerships, and you cannot ask to be a partner. These relationships are organic, similar to friendships, and are created over time. Treat everyone you work with as a friend and a partner, always keeping their best interests in mind, and you will have many opportunities to create partnerships with many different firms. Work to build their business, and your business will improve in turn.

Prospecting and Finding New Work

Prospecting is any activity that involves mining your current network for work. Regardless of how successful you've been with your advertising and marketing activities, how vast your network is, and how much high-quality work you have done, there will come times when you feel that you need to go out and find new opportunities. To work with the analogy of prospecting, think of your network as a vein of gold. There are some parts of the vein that have an abundance of easily obtained gold, while other parts of the vein are difficult to get to, or expensive to extract gold from. Occasionally veins run dry, and you have to find new veins to work with. Other times, old veins that had seemingly run dry now have an abundance of gold in them waiting to be collected. The analogy is strong, and it is fitting to think of your network in this fashion.

The best time to engage in prospecting is while you are still actively engaged in billable work. Routinely gauge the health of your business and the state of your upcoming workload so that you know when things are beginning to slow to a point where it is time to look for new work. At such times, get your hands dirty and go prospecting for new clients and projects. You can start with mining your known network. As you dig through your contacts and reach out to people, invariably new contacts will surface and your network will widen.

■ **Rule**   The truly successful prospector is one who is constantly searching. If you are continually looking for new opportunities and mining your network, you will have far greater success finding work than if you engage in it only when you truly need the work.

To have the highest success rate and quickest results from prospecting, contact everyone you know. Ask them if there is anything you can help out with, and let them know you are available. You will be amazed how quickly you can find work simply by asking for it. You don't want to use this tactic all of the time, and there are various ways that you can phrase your message so that you don't sound like you are begging, but the more dire the circumstances, the more forward you should be in your request. As you contact people, make sure you offer them something—a free lunch, an in-person meeting, a copy of your latest book, an introduction to a new resource or skill that you have— whatever you can think of to make the conversation about more than just a request for work.

Rule   Cold calling is not an activity you should engage in as an independent service provider. Some people, when considering how to find new work, immediately conclude they need to cold-call potential clients to create work. This is not true for the type of work you are doing. Expanding your business should be based on intelligent networking, aligning yourself with strategic partners, and utilizing your advertising and marketing material.

Converting Prospects to Sales

Your networking, advertising, and prospecting work will result in leads coming to you. If you have attracted these leads through these channels, these leads will be warm and ready to engage with you. Converting that desire to engage into an actual paid engagement, though, can often be a process that requires thoughtful negotiation. The following list outlines several techniques that you can use to convert the lead into a sale.

Rule   Because the sales cycle often takes a very long time, it is critical that you have many leads and potential opportunities in the queue at the same time. Never assume that a promising lead will close tomorrow, or that a paid project will materialize when you need it to. Work with every lead and nurture all of your business relationships, as you never know which will close tomorrow or who will need your services a year from now.

---

1. **Sell while on the phone.** Be prepared to talk numbers and reach an agreement during a phone call. Don't be afraid to give ballpark estimates on-the-fly, and never hesitate to throw out a number (see "Pricing Strategies" later in the chapter). The tendency is to talk through the scope of work and then tell the prospect that you will get back to them after you've had a chance to figure out the price. What you really need to do is talk through everything while you are on the phone, and drive to conclusion.

2. **Visit the prospect in person.** You will find that some potential clients simply cannot make a decision. They really want to do work with you, but something is preventing them from pulling the trigger and moving forward. It could be that they are part of a business culture that is simply slow to move. It could be that they are not the true buyer, but have to get approval from someone else. It could be any number of things, and you need to find out what it is. The easiest way to find out and to be able to address it head-on is to visit the prospect in person.

3. **Follow up and remain present.** Make sure to keep in contact with your leads. Send e-mails checking on status. If too much time elapses between conversations, you will become less relevant to them.

■ **Rule** The sales process will give you a lot of insight into the client. A simple and efficient sales cycle will lead to client work that is rewarding, easy to deliver on, and pays well. A difficult and drawn-out sales cycle generally ends with a client relationship that is poor and work that is taxing.

---

4. **Offer an incentive.** Sometimes it can help push someone to decision by offering an incentive that can't be refused. "If you sign up today, I can give you a discount of 10% on the monthly fee." Your prices are largely arbitrary, and you can make a profit at virtually any price, so bring some flexibility into conversations where you want to close business.

5. **Create new offerings.** As you are discussing needs and opportunities, talk with the potential client about additional offerings that may be of interest to them. Discuss the option of bringing additional resources in to deliver on a broader scope of work. Let the prospect know not only that you can help with the specific piece of work on offer, but that you also have skills that would enable you to tackle other things related to it.

CASE STUDY

A project was coming to a close with a major client, and I really wanted to figure out how to continue to work with them. At the close of the project, I offered two resources (contractors that I work with). I offered the first at an hourly rate, and told them that if they wanted the second resource, both would be discounted. The client decided additional resources at those prices were a great deal, and extended the project and the relationship. The client originally had no need for the additional resource until an offer that couldn't be refused was made.

Six Steps to Close a Sale

The following list of steps uses an example scenario to illustrate what you need to do to convert a lead into a sale. Although this list focuses on a specific example, knowing these steps and understanding how to quickly include them in your own conversations will better enable you to drive a conversation to a completed sale.

■ **Rule** Always negotiate as much as you can over the phone or in person. Never rely solely on e-mail, unless the prospective client simply won't pick up the phone.

---

1. **Initial conversation.** A prospective client reaches out to you and says they have a specific piece of work they need your help with. They tell you at a high level they want to build an integration between two systems, and need to pass account and contact information.

2. **Get basic scope.** You talk with the prospect over the phone and get more detail on the scope. You ask if they need testing, production deployment, documentation, and/or ongoing support. You ask enough detail about the project to determine if the scope is clear, or if more requirements gathering needs to take place.

3. **Present options.** On the same call, once you have a clear picture of what they are after, you present them with the following three options to engage (depicted in Figure 7-1):

    a. *Option 1*: A fixed price of $25,000 based on six weeks of work that covers just the portion of the work that was discussed.

b. **Option 2:** Includes option 1 but also bundles in three additional months of retainer support at $5,000 a month; it includes any activities related to production issues, bug fixes, or minor enhancements related to work done in the first option.

c. **Option 3:** A $7,500 a month retainer for six months, or $6,500 for twelve months; this final option includes all the work outlined in option 1 and option 2. It could also include additional project work as it comes up. The goal with option 3 is to create a long-term relationship with the client at a rate that will be sustainable for both parties.

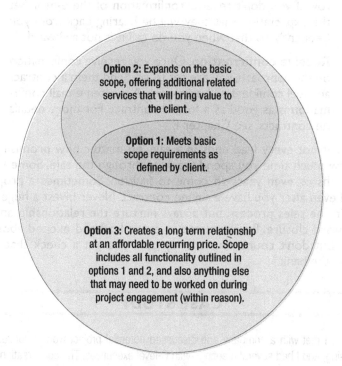

Figure 7-1. Each option offered should build on the previous option and expand value

Rule You may need to contract with the client for a simple hourly engagement to establish trust before you are able to present options that are based on different approaches. If you do decide to go hourly, make sure you limit it to a short, up-front engagement (four to six weeks maximum) and tell them that you will be revisiting the fixed and retainer models at a later time. See Chapter 9 for more details about different engagement models.

4. **Discuss the options.** With the options laid out to the prospect, let them respond. Get their feedback, and a sense of which direction they are leaning. Usually they will respond about scope, as your fees should be in line or lower than most other providers can offer. In your discussion, address any concerns they have. See which option matches their needs best. Come to a verbal agreement on which approach seems most compelling.

5. **Seek confirmation via e-mail.** At the end of the call, tell the client that within the next hour or two you will send an e-mail to them with an outline of what you just discussed. Tell them you will follow up by phone tomorrow if you don't receive confirmation of the e-mail. Set the expectation that they will be hearing back from you frequently, so that when you do call it is not awkward.

6. **Receive confirmation.** Once you receive confirmation on the approach, you are set to go. Send them a contract and feel confident to begin work. A written e-mail confirmation is as good as a formal contract. For more details on contracts, see Chapter 8.

Realize that not every lead ends in a sale, no matter how promising it may be or how much time you spend working through the sale. Some leads can take months or even years to come to fruition. Sometimes a project gets canceled even after you have a signed contract. Never invest a huge amount of time in the sales process, but always nurture the relationship and try to work toward closure. Be interested in every lead and excited about every contract, but don't count your money until you get a check that you can deposit in the bank.

CASE STUDY

In 2004, I met with a company and discussed potential project work. It looked very promising, and I had several meetings with C-level executives. The conversations died out, and I did not hear back from anyone. Late in 2007, one of the executives called me and asked if I might be able to come to his office for a conversation. I met with him in person, and within a few months I had a small contract. This small contract turned into a large one, and eventually into a long-term retainer that is still current. The sales cycle on this was almost four years, but the outcome was nearly seven years of constant recurring income.

Pricing Strategies

One of the most difficult aspects of selling services is to determine the appropriate fee. Chapter 9 details a variety of ways to set fees, and you should be confident in your fee structures before ever talking with a lead. There are several ways to estimate figures quickly while on the phone talking to a potential client and trying to close the deal. The following is a list of strategies you can use to calculate pricing. Discuss your pricing verbally, either on the phone or in person, so that you can sense the prospect's reaction and adjust your approach accordingly.

1. **Ask the prospective client what the budget is.** Very few employees are comfortable talking about price, largely because they are not used to talking about the high numbers that are usual in the technology industry. You will find that many people you negotiate with are also reluctant to share budget constraints, and want you to give a number first so that they can privately assess it. It is up to you how you want to play the game, but the more you can control the conversation, the better the chance you will end up with a sale and a situation that is of value to both you and the client. The easiest thing to do is to ask the prospect what they envision the budget to be, and what they feel a sustainable rate is.

CASE STUDY

I had been working with a client on scoping out and pricing a major piece of development, and had given a variety of options and prices on how to engage. The person I was working with was not the buyer, so he had to take everything back to his manager to get approval. I was growing weary with the process, and had decided they wouldn't be moving forward when they called me and said they had gotten an estimate from another vendor to do a small portion of the project. I said, "Tell me the ballpark budget they gave you, and I will tell you if I can do it for that price." They gave me the estimate, I told them I could do it for that price, and the sale closed that afternoon.

---

2. **Compare the cost of working with a larger firm.** The billing rates for consultants and contractors vary widely. The rates generally are $25 to $50 an hour for offshore resources, $60 to $90 an hour for contractors working in the United States, and $110 to $180 an hour for resources through staffing firms and consulting firms. The final rate depends on the specific technology being used and the requirements for onsite vs. offsite work. Knowing these rates, you should be able to quickly figure what it would cost for your client to do work with others. For example, you can say to them, "For this six-week engagement, you would be paying $38,400 for a single resource from a large consulting firm. Not only am I more qualified to do the work, but I can do it for a fixed cost of $25,000."

■ **Rule** You need to be comfortable stating prices and giving estimates. Saying that your rate is $80 an hour and leaving it at that is not your path to success, and doesn't assist the potential client in figuring out how best to engage on the project. Provide some context for your rate, and, if at all possible, try to give them an idea of what something will cost before you start on it.

---

3. **Offer incentives for a larger engagement.** If a client is willing to take on more resources that come from your team, you can always lower your prices. You can also offer a discount if the scope of work is greater. For example, your rate may be $9,000 a month for three months, $7,500 a month for six months, or $6,500 a month for a year's commitment. The Chapter 8 section "Pricing Strategies" has more information on this.

4. **Keep prices low and highly competitive.** In many cases, your client will be a consulting or staffing firm that has hired you to work on a project for one of their clients. Pricing in this situation is different from pricing directly with a client, because in this case you must make sure you quote a rate that allows the firm to make a profit. Large firms have huge overhead. If they are billing $180 an hour, for example, they typically can't pay more than $70 an hour to a subcontractor. In certain cases, such as where the firm has already committed to a client that they will

provide a resource, you have more room for negotiation, but your goal here should be to come up with a mutually agreeable rate that will enable you to sustain your relationship with and receive work from the firm on a continual basis and on a variety of projects. Keep your prices low, and you will have constant work.

■ **Rule** Subcontractors can make a nice income by engaging with a single client, but this is not the path to wealth and independence; it leaves too much up to chance and uncertainty, and limits freedom, growth, and potential.

CASE STUDY

There is a large network of independent contractors who take on short-term contracts with one client at a time. These contracts may last three months or longer, and generally pay between $60 and $90 an hour. These almost always require full-time, onsite commitment, with the contractor being responsible for living and travel expenses. In almost every case, these individuals live in the "feast or famine" scenario. When they have a project, they have their feast, but when the project ends, they are seeking work, and often have a period of time with no work (the famine). Being in business for yourself, you should never have a famine. You can structure your workload and your sales activities such that you always have a feast, and those infrequent times of lower activity are still supported with high income through long-term retainers.

The Sales Plateau

As you build your practice and sell work, you will find that your sales can generally be traced to plateaus of income. For example, when starting out, you may have a sales income of $15,000 a month. This income will remain fairly static, regardless of what projects you are working on or what client is paying you. You'll have a few weeks or months in which you may have more income temporarily, but your income will rarely (if ever) drop below this value. This $15,000 income is a plateau. Eventually, with your sales, network, marketing, and advertising, you will grow to the next plateau of income, where once again you will reach a point at which your income rarely falls below the plateau, and you have occasional periods in which it peaks above it. Figure 7-2 shows a sample illustrating this paradigm.

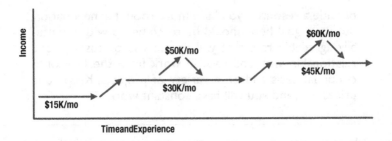

Figure 7-2. The sales plateau paradigm

You will know you have reached a plateau when you have several months with a consistent income above a certain point. This is your best model for forecasting what your income will be in the future. When you have identified the current plateau's value, you can make financial plans and do things with your money with the confidence that the coming months will have the same income, even though you cannot prove it in advance. As an independent businessperson, you should find it extremely easy to manage your financial picture and expectations using this approach.

Rule   You can rely on these plateaus to stay steady, as long as you are doing all of the relevant work related to keeping your business healthy. If you ever fall below your plateau, treat it as a red flag, and know that you have not been investing enough time in advertising, marketing, networking, or closing sales.

Balancing Sales with Delivery

Networking, prospecting, and closing sales all must be done while you continue to deliver on your project commitments. If you want a thriving business, you have to learn to balance your delivery activity with your sales activity. You will always have pressure to deliver on your projects, but your priority should always be to make time to sell. If someone wants to discuss buying your services for a project, make that your priority.

A sales call usually takes only a few minutes, and won't jeopardize your ability to deliver on your projects. Delivery work, on the other hand, is a constant and will always be there. When you are in business for yourself, whether you are a small-time contractor who engages on a single project at a time or a thriving private practitioner who has multiple active engagements, in every situation the potential sale is a higher priority than delivery work.

CASE STUDY

I was performing technical interviews with several candidates for a long-term contract with a client. The first candidate had come highly recommended, and was the most likely person to get the job. The candidate's current project was ending in a week, and this new contract was to start immediately after. We scheduled a time to do a technical interview. Fifteen minutes before the scheduled interview, the candidate sent an e-mail asking to reschedule, saying that he was caught in a production deployment scenario and couldn't step away. I went on to interview another candidate later that afternoon, and that second candidate got the job. I didn't bother speaking to the first candidate who couldn't step away from the production support issue.

Conclusion

To have successful sales as a solo practitioner in the technology field, you need to master the sales process, but you do not need to be a salesperson. You need to look at yourself as a service provider who knows how to sell, and is comfortable in negotiations. To sell, you have to have a network of clients, colleagues, and partners. You have to mine this network constantly for opportunities for yourself, and also opportunities to give to people in this network. If you are constantly engaging with and growing your network, you will have a steady flow of leads coming to you. Converting these leads into sales requires that you are able to think quickly and converse intelligently during phone calls, and define scope and pricing options. You have to be willing to work with every lead, but not every lead turns into a client. If you practice patience, balance your delivery work with your sales work, and are confident and realistic in your pricing, you will have a thriving practice and a full pipeline of future opportunities.

Proposals and Contracts

Trust, Simplicity, and Getting Paid

When the use of coin had once been discovered, out of the barter of necessary articles arose the other art of money-making, namely, retail trade; which was at first probably a simple matter, but became more complicated as soon as men learned by experience whence and by what exchanges the greatest profit might be made.

—Aristotle, *Politics*

This chapter deals specifically with proposals and contracts related to project engagement. It does not cover contracts you need to have to work with contractors and employees (see Chapter 11 for that) or details about contractual requirements for certain lines of business (for example, to be HIPAA compliant, you must have several types of paperwork in place). A proposal solidifies scope, while a contract formalizes an agreement.

This chapter recommends a minimalist approach to both proposals and contracts, placing ultimate reliance on trust, simplicity, and getting paid. In client relationships, you need to trust people. Before you write a contract, discuss the terms and scope with the client until you reach a mutually acceptable agreement, and then write the contract to include only the terms and scope that were agreed to. With respect to getting paid, work to create the most pay-friendly environment as possible, and do everything you can to get payment up front and on a recurring basis.

The Proposal Process

You will hear the line "Send me your proposal" frequently when negotiating business. Don't take the traditional course of working through a detailed write-up of the work and sending a written proposal to the client. Instead, immediately respond with, "We can discuss proposed ways of working together right now." Every proposal you give should always be discussed over the phone (or in person). You want to discuss and negotiate scope, resourcing, timing, and pricing in real time with clients, so that when it's time to write the actual contract, you are working with a solid base and there are no surprises or negotiations left.

■ **Rule** There is a great deal of overlap between the proposal process and the sales process. Review Chapter 7 for more details on selling.

Your proposal process should never end in a written proposal; rather, it should end in a written contract or statement of work (SOW). If you have not reached an agreement over the phone and via e-mail about what the terms of the project are, you need to continue the dialogue until you have reached an agreement. Verbal discussions are best, as you can sense what direction to take, immediately respond to concerns, and negotiate a proper outcome. You can't do these things effectively when sending a formalized written proposal via e-mail. If you jump straight to the written proposal and overprice your approach or misjudge what services to provide, you run the risk of offending the client and losing the work, even though you would have been more than happy to discuss alternative approaches. What you can propose easily and seamlessly in an interactive conversation that enables you to make quick adjustments can be off-putting if proposed initially via e-mail or other written means.

■ **Rule** Put as little time and effort into paperwork as possible, and never spend time on a complex Request for Proposal (RFP) or other major deliverables related to the sales process. Large firms have employees who specialize in preparing RFPs and similar documents, whereas you do not. You, as an independent businessperson focused on wealth and independence, have better things to do with your time than lengthy exercises with paperwork. Either someone wants to engage with you, or you need to cut them loose. The only formal paperwork you should ever do related to project engagements is the final contract.

Knowing that the proposal process is completely based on an active and ongoing conversation, you need to be able to drive the client to agreement. The components that you must agree on before you close the conversation are outlined in the following list. With practice, your skill at negotiation, defining scope quickly, and offering costs and timelines will improve.

1. **Agree on scope and deliverables.** The scope discussed should cover what the client needs you to do. Do not get carried away with minutiae while defining scope, and do not create deliverables for yourself that are irrelevant to the job at hand. For example, if the scope of work is an integration between system A and system B, you need to discuss scope specific to error handling, retries, entity structures, mapping, and all code and testing related to this. What you do not need to do is say that you'll put together a project plan, status reports, or any other incidental paperwork that should be handled by someone else (unless you are going to bill extra for it). You do not need to write numerous pages of information detailing how you will do the work, or what the limits of the work will be. You simply need to agree on the high-level deliverables, and account for the details in your timeline and pricing.

■ **Rule** You should be able to define scope in a few bullet points and sentences. Big organizations get overly detailed about what will be delivered. You need to remain agile and flexible, and must be easy to do business with, so your written SOWs need only set general parameters.

---

2. **Agree on level of effort.** After you have defined scope, reach agreement on the amount of work there is to do. You should be able to give solid, ballpark estimates instantaneously. For example, if someone asks you to build an application, you should immediately be able to say something like, "That is six weeks of work for one person, so two people could complete it in three weeks." Be honest in your discussions, and make sure the client is comfortable with the resourcing needs. Account for what you know will be required to deliver a quality solution, include some buffer to allow for minor scope changes, and proceed.

3. **Agree on cost**. After you have agreed on the resourcing needs, discussing cost is pretty straightforward. If it is six weeks of work, then you can base the cost on a variety of things, but generally speaking the cost is anywhere from $9,600 (based on $60/hr fulltime in a month) to $28,800 (based on $180/hr fulltime in a month), and you can determine where to price it based on several factors. Those factors include the amount of work you'll have to do, how difficult or specialized the work is, and the amount of value you ultimately bring to the client. If it is very difficult or highly specialized work, base your cost on the top-end pricing. If it is something you can do rapidly and easily, base your cost on the lower end with the expectation that you will deliver a higher-quality product in less time and at a lower cost. See Chapter 7 and Chapter 9 for more details on how to price your services.

4. **Agree on timing**. Try to start as soon as possible. You should be able to take on multiple projects simultaneously, so you should never be in a position of saying, "I can't start on this for four to six weeks." If the client asks if you can start next week and you are packed solid with work, start ramping up on the project next week. If you are serious about your goals and the success of your independent business, you will figure out a way to deliver on it, regardless of your workload.

5. **Agree on next steps**. Figure 8-1 is an example of an e-mail that summarizes a proposal that was discussed on the phone, along with several options that were outlined during the call. An e-mail summary is the most formal presentation you will need to make during the proposal process, and is the last step prior to documenting everything in your contract (or simply sending an invoice to the client to get work started). By the close of the proposal process, you should be very clear about what you are doing, when you are starting, and how much you will be paid. You only need a simple verbal or written response that everything is inline before you send your contract.

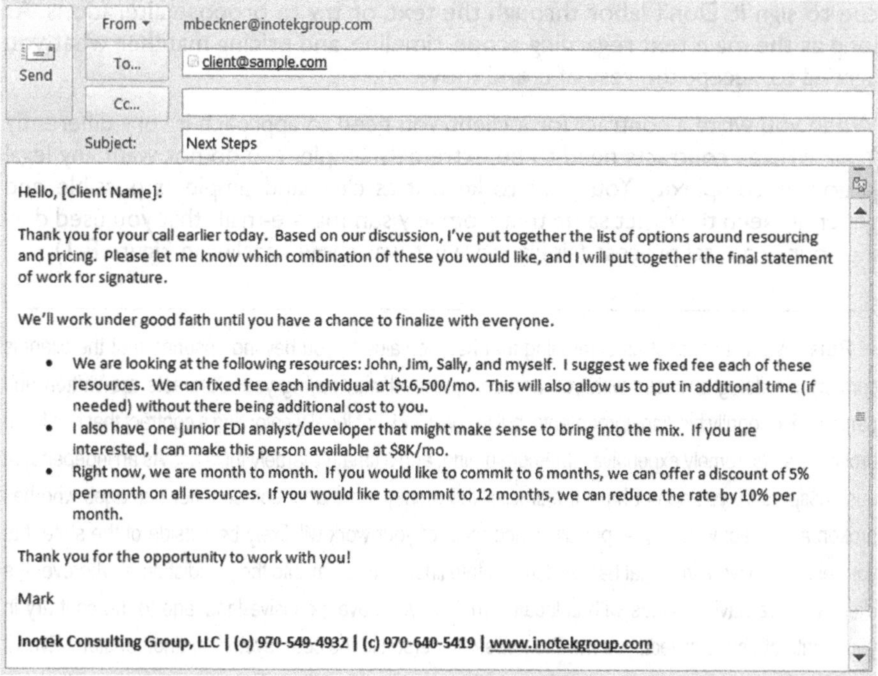

Figure 8-1. E-mail, the only format that you will ever need for a written proposal

As soon as you have reached agreement on these components, you can take action. You should have a proposal that can be easily documented in an e-mail for validation. Perhaps you have several open items that the client needs to decide on, or maybe you are ready either to sign the client's contract or write a contract for the client to sign. In either case, you have worked through the entire proposal process while in conversation with the client. You have never presented them with something that hasn't already been discussed, and at no time have you delivered any paperwork beyond an e-mail summarizing your approach.

The Contract Process

You need to be familiar with two types of contracts: contracts that you write in order to work with your clients, and contracts that your clients write in order to work with you. When a client writes a contract for you, it generally means they have a legal team and stringent guidelines for working with contractors or subcontractors; these contracts are usually lengthy and complex, and are not open for negotiation. In many cases, you will write the summary of your deliverables and send this to the client, which in turn will paste it into their template and ship it back to you for review and signature. This is your cue to sign it. Don't labor through the text, or try to propose alterations. As long as the main text regarding scope, timeline, and pricing matches what you agreed to, accept the rest of it and move on.

When you write a contract for a client, you need to approach it very differently. Your written contracts need to be extremely simple. You do not want any legal jargon or complexity. You want to keep it as clear and simple as possible, and generally keep the exact same text from any summary e-mails that you used during your proposal process (similar to what was shown earlier in Figure 8-1).

Rule   View a contract as something that has no value to you beyond ensuring that the client is comfortable doing business with you and can proceed with paying you. Contracts are written and perceived as legally binding agreements, but you will find that legally enforcing a contract that has been broken is an extremely expensive, time-consuming, and ultimately largely futile act. As an independent businessperson, you do not have the time or the money to go after someone for damages who has broken a contract with you, especially since most of your work will likely be outside of the state that you reside and work in. Legal battles across state lines usually fall into the jurisdiction of wherever the client you are having issues with is located (unless you have extensive language to the contrary in your contract), so to collect, you have to appear in person in the court system of another state. Even if you do win your court case, you then have to figure out how to collect. There is no guarantee that you will get paid, even after investing time and money and winning a case. It is an unfortunate truth that laws are written largely to protect the criminal. In general, you are better off focusing on new revenue streams and writing off your loss as a cost of doing business than trying to collect what is rightfully yours. Learn to collect your pay up front, and work to get paid. Stop working immediately if you are not paid on time, so that you are never owed a huge amount by a single client.

Any contract you write should be short and extremely basic. Everything you include in the contract should be what has already been agreed to verbally during the proposal and sales process. There is no need to add legal wording, and there is only negative value in adding penalty clauses. A contract for you is literally just another component of the process of making a client feel comfortable paying you, and ensuring everything is in place for them to do business with you.

How to Write a Contract

You do not need a lawyer to write a contract for you. Your contracts should be as simple as possible. You do not want heavy legal language that might deter a client from doing business with you. You want a simple agreement that anyone can understand and that no one can argue with. Target one or two pages at most, and include the key elements outlined in the following list. If you keep a reusable template and have worked through the proposal process correctly, it should take you no more than half an hour to write up the final contract and send it to your client.

1. **Name and location.** Specify that the contract is between you and the client. Include appropriate addresses. Don't list your home address if you work out of your home. Use a post office box or other external address. Always keep your person separate from your business (see Chapter 5 for more details).

2. **Scope of work.** This is the summary of what you will be working on. This scope of work should be bullet points that outline specific tasks that you have discussed with the client during the proposal process. If you have validated the scope verbally, as recommended, simply list the items that you have agreed upon. If you have validated scope via e-mail, then copy the contents from the e-mail in which the client agreed to the scope and paste it directly into the contract.

Rule If you can't summarize scope in a short summary paragraph with a few bullet points (even for fixed-fee projects), then you need to rethink your scope. For hourly and retainer work, the scope should be very high level; for example, "Help out in any way needed as related to build out of SQL integration." For a fixed-fee project, you should be able to summarize the whole deliverable with something similar to "Develop and test EDI maps for purchase order integration with up to five external trading partners. Production deployment and support is not included. Documentation is not included."

---

3. **Client responsibilities.** Outline what is required from the client for you to succeed. Usually this just means the client must be available to discuss project details, but occasionally you will need the client to provide sample data or take part in testing for you to be able to complete your portion of the project. Often, a client will assume that you'll take on everything related to a solution, even though you have specifically stated you will be doing only development and unit testing. Judge the nature of your client, and include as much or as little detail in this section as you think is necessary.

4. **Schedule.** State when the work will commence and when it will end (if there is an end date). Sometimes it takes a while for a client to sign a contract, so giving a start date of something along the lines of "Work will commence on or before July 1, 2015" leaves it generic enough that you won't have to revise the contract just to correct the date when the client is finally ready to sign.

5. **Compensation.** This includes the fee and the payment terms. Specify clearly the date on which you intend to send the first invoice. In most cases, you will want to invoice when the project commences, but in some cases you will have to wait until the end of a month during which work has been performed. See the "Payment Strategies" section later in the chapter for ideas on how to approach this topic.

6. **Expenses.** If there are travel expenses associated with the project, state them in the contract. If there are incidental expenses (such as FedEx fees, etc.), just cover the cost yourself. In technology, expenses unrelated to travel are so rare that you should cover minor items on your own as part of your service.

These basic elements are consistent regardless of the type of contract you are putting together. The following subsections give example contracts for hourly, fixed-fee, and retainer-based work. Each of the examples includes the preceding basic elements, and each is approximately a page in length. You can model your contracts after these.

■ **Rule** In many cases you will not have to write a contract; your client will do this for you, as they have internal regulations on how to work with contractors. Do not try to negotiate the wording of a contract that a client asks you to sign. Check for major items such as the price, payment cycle, and start and end dates, but leave the rest as is. Many large firms have dozens of pages of legal stipulations (noncompete clauses, ownership of work rules, nondisclosure agreements, etc.) that you will have no authority to change. Either you agree, or you don't work on the project. If you get in the business of negotiating the fine print of contracts, you need to stop being a coder and start attending law school.

Hourly Contracts

In cases where you are doing hourly work, the client is concerned more about your time than a specific cost. Do everything in your power to create an agreement that guarantees a minimum number of hours each week, regardless of your utilization. Pure hourly contract work is the worst kind of relationship for both you and your client, and should be used only in cases where no other alternative is available (see Chapter 9 for more details on this). Most clients will be amenable to a set number of hours per week, and will understand that this will allow you to schedule your time and treat them with priority. Figure 8-2 shows an example of an actual fixed hourly contract.

This Statement of Work is between Inotek Consulting Group, LLC, with address of P.O. Box 2185, Grand Junction, Colorado 81502, and [Client Name] with offices located at [Client Address]. Both parties agree to the following terms and agreements.

I. Scope

This is a simple hourly engagement that covers all work associated with Architecture, Development, Design, Documentation and related activities. Resources may include Mark Beckner and [Subcontractor], but may be extended depending on appropriate skills and availability.

II. Terms and Conditions

- Project will begin on or around September 2nd, 2014.

- The hourly rate will be $65 for Mark Beckner, and $50 for [Subcontractor Name].

- 20 hours minimum per week will be billed by Mark Beckner. 40 hours minimum per week will be billed by [Subcontractor Name].

- Project will be invoiced at the end of each month. Payment will be due within 15 days from the time of invoicing.

This statement of work is accepted and forms agreement between the parties.

Inotek Consulting Group, LLC	[Client Name]
Signature: _____	Signature: _____
Name: Mark Beckner	Name: _____
Date: 8/29/2014	Date: _____

Figure 8-2. Sample hourly contract

Retainer Contracts

Long-term retainers are your ideal client relationship. These allow for ongoing work without being tied to specific hours or deliverables. If you price yourself right, are extremely good at what you deliver, and show the value of the relationship to the client, you will have no trouble selling a retainer-based project. Retainers allow for higher quality work from you at a cost that is often less than an employee (which is a miracle within the world of contract-based

IT resources), and gives assurance to the client that you are available and will be around for the long term. A fairly priced retainer with a good client can last for years.

When writing up your retainer contract, keep the scope at a very high level, and try not to commit to specific deliverables. Think of yourself as an employee who is there to help out with whatever comes along. If the work ever becomes too much of a load for the price given, have a conversation with the client and explain how the amount of work exceeds the spirit and scope of the retainer, and either change the model or help the client to find additional resources. Figure 8-3 is an example of a retainer-based contract.

Consultant Work Order

Consultant Name: Mark Beckner performing services for Inotek Consulting Group, LLC

Client Name & Location: [Client Name and Location]

Scope of work: Services shall be provided remotely, in a retainer model, which will include (but is not limited to):

- BizTalk support as required by Client
- Scope of work will be jointly determined by Client & Sr. BizTalk Architect
- Full time estimation for given tasks will be discussed and agreed to by both parties
- Client will have full access to Sr. BizTalk Architect by email & phone
- Sr. BizTalk Architect will respond immediately to any request

Client responsibilities and prerequisites include: Insuring the availability of key personnel.

Work Schedule: As required by the Client.

Compensation: The Consultant will invoice a retainer fee of $5,500 (Five Thousand Five Hundred Dollars) per month for 12 months (billed monthly).

Anticipated Start Date: December 21st, 2013

Expected Project Termination Date: On or about December 21st, 2014

Expenses/Costs: No expenses incurred by the Consultant in connection with the provision of services to the Client are to be reimbursed. This is remote work, and no onsite travel will be performed.

AGREED TO BY THE PARTIES BELOW:

_____	_____	_____
Client Name	Title	Date
_____	_____	_____
Inotek Consulting Group	Title	Date

Figure 8-3. Sample retainer contract

Sample Fixed-Fee Contract

Contracts for fixed-fee projects require more structure than is required for retainer and hourly contracts. You need to clearly outline the boundaries of your scope of work. With retainers and hourly work, you want to be very general, but with fixed fees you must specify exactly what components you will develop and what portions of the project life cycle you will engage in (unit testing, production deployment, documentation, etc.). Keep the scope brief, but make sure that it stipulates what your commitments are and where your work ends.

In some cases, you may want to reference an external spreadsheet or other document that details the specific deliverables. These documents may have been provided to you during the proposal process (many clients will shop various service providers using documentation outlining what they believe the scope is), or they may be collateral material you used during informal talks with the client. In either case, you can certainly include them in your contract. Figure 8-4 is an example of a fixed-fee contract that references a spreadsheet (not shown) with more detail on deliverables.

[Client Name/Project]

This Statement of Work is between **Inotek Consulting Group, LLC**, with address of P.O. Box 2185, Grand Junction, Colorado 81502, and **[Client Name]**, with offices located at [Client Address]. Both parties agree to the following terms and agreements.

I. Scope

Development, testing and deployment to production of BizTalk maps as specified in MapList.xlsx. No development of SQL or other components that are not specifically BizTalk maps or C# reference libraries required by the maps.

II. Terms and Conditions

- All maps to be completed by 12/31/2014

- Payment Schedule will be
    o Phase 1- $8,000.00 – 9/15/2014 (Billing Date)
    o Phase 2- $8,000.00 – 10/1/2014 (Billing Date)
    o Phase 3- $8,000.00 – 11/1/2014 (Billing Date)
    o Phase 4- $8,000.00 – 12/1/2014 (Billing Date)
    o Final Payment: $12,000.00 – 1/1/2015 (Billing Date)
    Total: $44,000.00

III. Client Responsibilities

Client will be responsible for providing test data and validating output of maps.

This statement of work is accepted and forms agreement between the parties.

Inotek Consulting Group, LLC	**[Client Name]**
Signature: _____	*Signature:*_____
Name: *Mark Beckner*	*Name:*_____
Date: *8/29/2014*	*Date:*_____

Figure 8-4. Sample fixed-fee contract

Invoicing

The purpose of proposals and contracts is to make your client comfortable working with you. Invoicing is the final step in the process, and states that actual payment is due. Being paid on an invoice is infinitely better than getting a signature on a contract, and in many cases is all that you need to get paid. Do not ever think that you need a contract to start working. If the person you are talking to agrees to your scope and ends the call with "send me an invoice," you should immediately send an invoice and get to work. In many cases, clients neither need nor want a contract. You'll find that in many situations an invoice serves as a contract, and you don't need anything more.

CASE STUDY

Many clients will work with you without a contract. Many buyers have access to funds that they can use in any way they see fit within their silo of business. For example, they can purchase hardware or services for IT-related work to improve their business. What they cannot do is sign contracts. If they receive a contract, they have to take it to their legal team to get it verified; once something goes to a legal team, it can take weeks before a heavily revised version is returned.

In much of my client work, I agree to terms and conditions over the phone, and then send an invoice immediately after the call for the scope of work discussed. If I have established verbally that I will be working with the client for six months at $7,500 a month, I send an invoice for the first month and begin work, almost always without a contract.

If a client requests a contract, I put one together (see samples of these contracts earlier in this chapter). If a client requires that I sign one of their contracts before moving forward, I sign whatever they send over.

Your invoices need to be timely and professional. You should use a standard accounting application that other service firms use (QuickBooks Online is a good option), and always send your invoice with a personal e-mail thanking the client for the work. Your invoice also needs to be simple to read. Figure 8-5 is an example of an invoice.

Inotek Consulting Group, LLC
P.O.Box 2185
Grand Junction, CO 81502

(970)640-5419
mbeckner@inotekgroup.com
http://www.inotekgroup.com

Invoice

Date	Invoice No.
08/31/2014	▬▬▬

Terms	Due Date
Net 15	09/15/2014

Bill To

Date	Activity	Quantity	Rate	Amount
09/01/2014	Development Services, September 1 - 30, 2014 (Mark Beckner)	1	5,000.00	5,000.00
09/01/2014	▬▬▬▬ September 1 - December 31, 2014 (Prepayment discount @ $4000/Month)	4	4,000.00	16,000.00
			Total	$21,000.00

Figure 8-5. Sample invoice

Rule Many developers create their own custom invoices and manage their money in a spreadsheet. One of your goals is to sustain a high income, so buy the tools needed to support that goal. A $400 annual license for high-grade accounting software that is easy to use is a tiny investment for someone who should be making an absolute minimum of $250,000 a year.

Send your invoices the moment they are due. If you told your client that you would bill at the end of the month, send your invoice on the last day of the month. Never postpone your invoicing. The longer you wait to invoice, the longer the client will wait to pay you.

Payment Strategies

Receiving payment from your client is the only definitive proof that the client is committed to working with you. Your goal in putting together the payment or pricing plans is to figure out how to get paid in the quickest way possible, to establish the client's commitment. The following list outlines several approaches to getting paid in an expedited manner; some of them even allow openings for greater income. There are many more. Be creative, and think of things that may appeal to your specific client.

1. **Seek advance payment.** When you are engaging in a fixed-fee or retainer-based project, you can easily require an up-front payment as part of the agreement. For example, if the client has committed to a retainer of $8,500 a month for six months, you can bill the first $8,500 at the start of the month rather than at the end. Or, if the client has committed to a fixed-fee project for $50,000, you can create a payment timeline that includes a portion of the fee up front. Note that getting advanced payment on hourly projects is extremely difficult.

Rule You are not in the business of financing projects for your clients. If you take the traditional payment approach, you will be floating costs for one to three months before you get paid. For example, if the project starts September 1, you invoice on September 30, and there is a 45-day pay period, you'll have to wait 75 days to get paid for your initial work. That is a long time to float money for a client, but it is very common. In cases where you are working directly with clients, you should be able to expedite your cash flow (payment due in advance, for example). In cases where you are a subcontractor for a firm, you'll be largely at the mercy of their timelines, so there isn't much you'll be able to do here other than plan for delayed payment.

---

2. **Offer a discount for prepayment.** Offering your client a 15% discount on the overall cost of the project if they pay in full in advance may work for fixed-fee or retainer-based projects. Getting $50,000 today vs. $60,000 over the course of six or nine months is worth it. You don't have to worry about not getting paid, and you still get paid even if the project gets cancelled. Offer a sizeable enough discount to make it of interest to the client, but low enough that it is still of interest to you.

3. **Offer a discount if multiple resources are engaged.** You'll likely be working with subcontractors (and possibly employees; see Chapter 11), so you should be able to say in many cases, "My rate is $7,500 a month, but if you want two resources, I can drop my rate to $6,000 and you can have a second resource for $5,000." Think of how you are inclined to purchase simple products from the grocery store when you see "Buy one, get one 50% off." You can apply the same approach with your services.

■ **Rule** As you progress in your career, you will have more leverage in your pricing. Being brand new generally means you take what you need in order to eat. Being established with a large pool of work and projects means you can be more selective in your work and require more favorable options in getting paid.

Conclusion

This chapter outlined approaches for working through the proposal and contract processes. The purpose of the proposal process is to engage the client in discussing, negotiating, and determining the scope and approach of the project, and the process should never involve written documents until verbal agreement has been made. The contract process is to ensure that your client is comfortable doing business with you; you should not view the written contract as protection of any kind for you. Regardless of the work you have put into delivery, sales, proposals, and contracts, ultimately the only proof you have that anyone values you professionally is that you get paid. Take a minimalist view to everything related to paperwork, always strive to keep both your own and your client's best interests in mind, and become proficient at instantly negotiating scope and price. You'll find that proposals are intrinsic to the nature of the work you are doing, that contracts will always be signed if you have already agreed to scope, and that you can frequently get paid without ever putting anything in writing. Try to make doing business with you the "simple matter" that Aristotle wrote of in the opening quote to this chapter.

Fees and Income

Creating a High-Dollar Revenue Stream

The world is full of money. Some of that money has your name on it.
All you have to do is collect it. You have little time to waste.

—Felix Dennis, *How to Get Rich*

You can make your fortune in virtually any profession. The technical industry, however, has many more options than most other avenues. The ability to make a healthy income is available to virtually anyone in tech, and the abundance of work means many more individuals will be able to make a good living in the future. But although the industry lends itself to a plethora of high-paying jobs, the ability truly to set yourself apart and make enough of an income to attain the wealth, freedom, and independence you are capable of requires dedication, hard work, and a thoughtful and creative approach to determining fees and engaging on projects.

As a coder, you can easily make a low six-figure income within the first few years of your career. Moving up the ladder in this income, however, becomes exponentially harder as time goes on, and it flattens out if you are employed by another. You cannot grow rich working for someone else, and you certainly cannot grow your independence that way. If you want to expand and allow yourself to grow in opportunities and wealth, this independence from others is critical, and the need to work for yourself and create new business is essential. In doing so, you will open up the path to making substantially greater income than would ever be possible through employment by others, and will be part of the creation of new paths to wealth.

There are many factors in making your wealth through coding—learning to negotiate fees, finding good projects, acquiring and retaining clients—but the two most important factors are hard work and intense, focused thought. Working hard and efficiently, and having clear goals lay the foundation for all of the rest of the factors to occur. Hard work alone leads nowhere, and many heavy laborers across the world barely subsist. So, too, many thinkers exist with grand ideas and million-dollar schemes, but can't execute on anything and remain in poverty throughout their lives. It is the person who works hard and finds time to spend in thought to determine goals and ideals who will be able to progress far beyond standard boundaries. "Faith without works is dead," wrote the apostle James—meaning, in this case, thought without action or hard work without dreams results in nothing. Faith with works can produce miraculous results.

Although thought and labor combined are the two most important aspects to the generation of wealth, there are several other pragmatic activities required to elevate yourself to a level of income that allows for your full potential, growth, and freedom. These activities are outlined here at a high level, and are given more detailed analysis later in this chapter. They are as follows:

1. **Become comfortable with money.** You must become comfortable with the idea of making, having, and talking about money. Some people are natural businesspeople; talk of money and sales is second nature and it predominates their mind-set and interactions with the world. Most of us, however, have some level of distrust of money and of those with money. The negative connotations are forced on us by popular culture, by media, by philosophies, and by history. Before you can acquire wealth, you have to make sure your thinking is in line with the healthy acquisition of money, and that you don't have undue bias toward those who have become successful before you. It is one thing to say, "I want to earn more money"; it is another to believe it and be comfortable with it when it happens—for you and for others.

2. **Take every opportunity and keep as many avenues open as possible.** Ensure that you are allowing all opportunities to present themselves and that at no time are you accepting work at the expense of excluding

other work. You must look constantly at how to expand your network and your base of opportunity generation. You can engage simultaneously on multiple projects in the same manner that a lawyer can execute with multiple clients or a physician can accommodate multiple patients. Working exclusively on one project at a time caps your income and cripples your effectiveness.

3. **Know fee structures.** Determining the appropriate fee structure to put in place for a project is an acquired skill. The most simplistic approach is the basic hourly fee model, which has limitations and often raises ethical questions. It is best to stay away from this structure, unless no other options are available or unless you can engage in a "fixed hourly" model. The fixed-fee model is a great way to work and ensures both you and your clients know what the costs will be, but it requires some experience and forethought to get an appropriate price in place, and it comes with a greater level of risk. The retainer model is the ideal situation for the skilled coder and for the buyer. It allows for creative approaches to scoping, providing deliverables, resourcing, and pricing. In most situations, targeting this approach first is the most appropriate and brings the most value to you and your clients.

4. **Understand how to determine a fair price.** Coming up with a price that is best for you and your clients does not mean figuring out the highest dollar amount possible to charge. A rate that is sustainable leads to more work in the future and helps to ensure clients never decide to engage with you based solely on price. These are the keys to deciding a fair and equitable rate.

■ **Rule** Focusing on fees with clients and figuring out how to charge the highest rate is not a path to wealth or abundance. Focus first on the underlying ideas of money, the role it needs to play in your life, and what use you will make of your wealth. When you are ready, doors will open that allow you to engage on projects and set fees easily that are fair to both you and your clients.

---

5. **State your goals and intentions.** When there is a certain level of momentum around projects and income, you must state your goals and intentions. These goals must be thought out and made concrete. A year from now, you must be able to look back and determine whether you've been successful in reaching your goals. If you haven't, you must evaluate why. Without stating specifically what you are after, you only earn a fraction of what is possible to make in your current situation. Chapter 10 details goal setting and can help you state concrete objectives in terms of fees and income.

The following sections in this chapter outline the details of each of these aspects of income generation and look at specifics of how to set your fees with clients to maximize your income. The underlying truth is that you must first labor well, efficiently, and effectively, and think and assess constantly. Do not underestimate the importance of hard work and deep thought in your ability to succeed.

Get Comfortable with Money

"There is nothing wrong in wanting to get rich," wrote Wallace D. Wattles in the *Science of Getting Rich*. "The desire for riches is really a desire for a richer, fuller, and more abundant life; and that desire is praise worthy."

Many people, in business and in private life, are not comfortable with money—especially when it is in the hands of someone else. Generally speaking, everyone would like to have more abundance. Often, the people who are most focused on money are those who have the least of it. There has been a distrust of people with money since the dawn of time; the poor have always felt wronged by the rich.

The applied anger of the "have-nots" toward the "haves" is similar in nature to racism. To hate another because of what they have or the color of their skin is foolishness, and reduces the human experience to the most basic of topics. The idea that there is a difference between the 99% and the 1% is bumper sticker philosophy at its worst, and indulging in ideas that create separation, anger, and distrust is the true danger. Ideology, not riches, cause the pain and suffering so many attribute to a person of wealth.

Rule   The world needs the rich and the poor. "The poor will be with you always," stated Christ, and so, too, will the rich. If you have a path ahead of you that allows for riches, without the sacrifice of what is important and true, then follow it. If your path is one of poverty, take it and embrace it. For the coder who is employed by another, you must sit at your computer for a certain number of hours. If you can, in the same amount of time, make $100 or $100,000, the best use of your time is to make the $100,000. What you do with that money is the measure of you; there is no other measurement with which to be concerned. Function at your highest potential.

There are radicals who believe there is no ethical use of money—that it distorts and confuses relationships, stewardship, and the human endeavor. Societies have been based on the idea that money and ownership are flawed, and that the ideal is a world of communal living. There are even some who have given up money all together—See Mark Sundeen's *The Man Who Quit Money* (Riverhead, 2012)—in the hopes of setting an example for how we should interact. At the root of this is a mistaken understanding of where money comes from.

Underlying this dislike of people with money is the idea that somehow those with money are taking from those without. There is an idea that there is a finite pool of resources and a finite number of dollars, and that every dollar one person earns is a dollar that is taken away from someone else. This is a misapplication of the economic idea of the "zero-sum game," and is the cause for much of the incorrect attitude toward wealth. This idea applies to truly finite resources—and it is questionable whether anything is truly finite.

If there are four potatoes on the table and there are eight people sitting at the table, the four people who get the potatoes do so at the cost of taking directly from the four who get nothing. This is an extremely limiting approach to resources, and it assumes there are only four potatoes. The truth is, there are enough potatoes to feed the world, they just aren't on the plate; they are out in the world, waiting to be harvested.

With money, the same is true. There is an unlimited amount of riches; it is just a matter of finding the sources. The cash won't be delivered to us on a plate. We have to search it out. To look at people and think they are corrupt or flawed or criminal because they have more money is similar to looking at someone with beauty and accusing them of having made someone else ugly. In truth, if the beautiful person did not exist, the world would have less beauty in it; if the rich person did not exist, the world would have less money and less opportunity in it.

The zero-sum mentality is dangerous, and it depends entirely on local business and the cultural environment. In the world of business, where there is a free market, there is an element of creation; new ideas spawn new wealth, and new inventions open channels for new avenues of income. Even in the natural world, where extreme amounts of debate and fear center around there not being enough oil, water, lumber, and so on, to go around, there is often abundance where there should be loss. For example, even with the massive consumption of oil, we continue to find vast, new, and previously undiscovered deposits that allow for ever-expanding needs There are endless articles on this; The Motley Fool reported just a week's worth of significant finds in "Offshore Drilling: Big Oil Hits a Gusher of Oil and Gas Discoveries."[1] With the extensive cutting of trees for consumer products and housing, we have more available lumber than ever before. This abundance is true on the macro level, but not always on the micro level.

In environments where resources are managed wisely, abundance is available. In environments where corruption and poor management rule, resources are lacking, the wealthy take from the poor, and the masses are left in poverty; the zero-sum game is an accurate reflection of the state of affairs. The mistake is to assume this is true everywhere and to apply it to all people. In your case, you are working in the technical industry, which is new, innovative, and creative. From it, many new jobs are created, massive new wealth is born, and new avenues of opportunity are created. This is true whether operating in a First World environment or a Third World environment. In all things, look for the truth, and understand where you fit in the process. If you are making your money in technology, it is highly unlikely that the money you generate is coming out of the hands of any single person, or that you are taking something from someone else. In actuality, the opposite is most likely true. You are following opportunities that likely wouldn't exist unless you were there, and your activities are ultimately leading to the creation of new wealth and more opportunities for others.

Your goal should never be money directly; it should be wealth. Wealth consists of far more than money. (See Chapter 12 for more detail, but in short it includes discretionary time, an open mind, generosity, and abundance in everything you do.) Money is similar to energy. It contains potential that can be used for many things. Human nature is such that this money energy can magnify the good or bad of the individual using it. People who make a lot of money and spend it to the detriment of themselves or those around them may have more money than someone else, but they are far from being wealthy. People who make less money but create something new from it and invest it in, making a richer life for themselves and those around them, are wealthy, regardless of the specific amount of money earned.

---

[1] http://www.fool.com/investing/general/2014/10/26/offshore-drilling-big-oil-hits-a-gusher-of-oil-and.aspx.

CASE STUDY

At a group dinner one evening, a woman asked me what I did. I responded very briefly that I wrote code and helped to automate business systems. She immediately became confrontational and asked how I could live with myself, making a living off of putting other people out of work. I had never considered what I did to be controversial or something that reduced the number of available jobs. On the contrary, I told her, it seemed that in virtually every situation the projects and work that I did created more work and new lines of business and support. I realized, though, as she became more unpleasant and aggressive in her denunciation of my work—and technology in business in general—that she was looking at the situation from a poverty mentality, from the idea that we live in a zero-sum game economy. Her take was that every gain by one person was a loss by someone else—that there was a finite number of jobs, a limited pool of money, and there was only so much to go around. She was set in her ways, and her world was likely governed by this mentality, but my take on the world is very different—there is space to create, engaging and doing work creates more opportunities, there is abundance, and everyone can join the game and win if they have interest. Our approach to life has a major impact on the reality created around us.

Embrace your ability to generate income and to have a skill that allows for the creation of greater wealth than many could dream of, both for yourself and for those around you. Put any subconscious guilt behind you, and open yourself to being part of the flow of energy that allows for the proper use and generation of income. Money may be the root of many evils, but it is not evil in and of itself. People who are not prepared for it, who have not worked for it and generated it themselves are the true cause for concern. An electrical wire that falls from a pole into a pool of water can cause death to those who come near. The person who is prepared and who is generating the money should never be condemned. An electrical wire that is properly mounted can carry electricity far and wide, and can create opportunities and possibilities for those who can prosper from it.

Rule Never sacrifice your values for money and never live life solely for income. As you make more money, take more time for reflection to ensure your activities and patterns of engagement reflect your values (and ensure you have values to reflect on!) Again, James writes, "Come now, you who say, 'Today or tomorrow we will go to such and such a city, and spend a year there and engage in business and make a profit.' Yet you do not know what your life will be like tomorrow. You are just a vapor that appears for a little while and then vanishes away." Remember your mortality; maximize your profits, minimize your time expenditures, and know that wealth and freedom are not made purely of money.

Take Every Opportunity: Multiple Revenue Streams

Opportunities will present themselves, and you must be able to take them. When you are in business for yourself and you are looking at how to maximize your income and your efficiency, your goal should be to have many simultaneous projects you can support successfully and for which you can bill. When you are have an employee mind-set, you look for one opportunity, one job; the moment you get it, the job search ends and you dedicate your time to a single employer. When you are in the independent business mind-set, you are dedicated to finding as many clients as possible; the job search never ends and you are never dedicated to one client.

Your ability to make a high income is not directly dependent on the amount of money you charge, but rather on the number of projects that you can engage and deliver in parallel successfully. You should be putting a great deal of work into your sales and advertising, which means you should have a continual stream of potential work coming to you. Be in a position to take on all the work that comes your way. If you are a true expert in the technologies you deliver, then you can engage on many projects at the same time.

I'd like to stress this point. The way to create a high-dollar revenue stream for yourself in business is by working many projects in parallel, not by the actual dollar amount charged per project. Many companies make their revenue through low-margin sales on massive quantities of items. The markup is low, but the end income is high. You can follow in a similar vein in the services industry by offering more services to more customers while charging a fee that is highly competitive and extremely fair to your clients.

As Figure 9-1 shows, you can increase your income dramatically as the number of opportunities increase, even if you are in the early stages of building your expertise and experience. Fees do not have to be driven up to make this income increase. In fact, they can flatten out, and not increase at all year to year, and you can still increase your income. It is all about learning to be able to engage on multiple projects simultaneously and successfully.

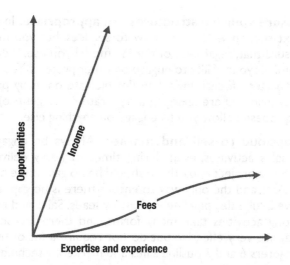

Figure 9-1. With expertise and opportunity, fees can flatline while income increases

---

■ **Rule** Many independent contractors speak of "feast or famine" with regard to work. Always be in the position of "feast." If you are doing things correctly in your independent business journey, there will never be a time when you do not have work. There are certainly ebbs and flows to the business cycle, and there will be times when large, high-revenue projects align to rocket you to the next level. But, the ebbs of the cycle are just that; even the lowest monthly income for you may look like a boon to anyone else. The way to ensure there is always a feast, and never a famine, is to have multiple clients and multiple projects, and many other opportunities in the queue. This is completely possible and is essential to your success.

Five Techniques for Delivering on Multiple Projects

The following list outlines the methods you can use to manage multiple projects.

1. **Manage your time.** Time management is the number one requirement for being able to engage successfully on multiple projects. No one client can consume all your time. Your skills must be such that you can deliver rapidly in anything you are producing. If you take on labor-intensive work, you may need to bring others onto your team (subcontractors) to deliver. Minimize time on calls and meetings. Always work to write code in a manner that is solid, solves the client need, and does not require an exorbitant amount of work to implement and test.

2. **Ensure your fee structures are appropriate.** In the next section we look at how to set fees, but you must ensure that, regardless of the fee model you use, it does not limit your ability to engage on other projects. You are far better off charging a low, flexible rate on many projects than you are charging a high rate on single project that doesn't allow you to engage on anything else.

3. **Continue to sell and market.** Always be engaged in sales activities, even during times of heavy delivery. When a project ends, there should be no gap to the next project, and the only way to ensure there is no gap is to have a full sales pipeline with many leads. Sales and marketing activities take many forms, and there are some that are very effective but do not require a lot of time. Chapters 6 and 7 outline sales and marketing techniques in more detail.

4. **Prioritize everyone.** When you are working with multiple clients, they must all be treated as if they are the only client you have. No client should ever be aware of what you are doing elsewhere, what other commitments you might have, and what your personal objectives are. Your client does not need to know your business, except as it relates to them; too much information can only hurt a relationship, never improve it. You should be ambiguous in everything. You should be honest and let your client know that you do have other work (this is a requirement of any independent contractor anyway), but it must be left at a very high level, and no specifics should be given. Make all your clients feel like they are your only client.

CASE STUDY

I had an excellent working relationship with a Texas company for several years. The work was interesting, the people were enjoyable, and the income was high. I had periodic onsite visits with them, and had been told the contract would be extended indefinitely. At one point, I had a business trip to Argentina and had to fly through Dallas. During the layover, I decided to visit with this client (rather than take a separate trip the following week). While onsite, they asked why I was coming a week early, and I foolishly mentioned I had a client in Argentina I was visiting for a couple of days. Within a few weeks, my Texas–based client ended my contract, and I never had work with that company again.

By providing visibility into some of the specifics of the other opportunities in which I was engaged, this client felt he was not the top priority, that I had other commitments of more importance. In truth, nothing had changed; I had engaged on multiple projects throughout the years I worked with them, but the client's perception had changed.

Always work to keep the details of what you are doing to yourself. A client is only concerned with his or her own interests, and should not be troubled or made aware of your interests. Tell the truth if asked directly, but remain as ambiguous as possible and never give too much detail.

---

5. **Master communication.** Your ability to communicate quickly and effectively is key to your ability to deliver on multiple projects and make everyone feel like they are a priority. Returning phone calls and responding to e-mail promptly are critical. Some developers limit their e-mail communications to "after hours," so that it doesn't affect their ability to concentrate on coding. Others go days at a time before responding to a query. These approaches are very damaging. You must be able to return an e-mail or phone call immediately during business hours. You don't have to address all the details, but you must respond and let the client know you received the communication and that you are looking into the best way to answer the question or deal with an issue. If the e-mail is in regard to the request of a deliverable, respond immediately with a time estimate of when you will be able to provide it. This takes only a moment, but it goes very far in keeping the relationship healthy and making the client feel valued.

Create Appropriate Fee Structures

There are several common approaches to fee structures that you can incorporate into your business in creative ways that allow you to make the outcome greater than the sum of its parts. Your goal should always be to figure out a fee structure that leaves you with the flexibility to engage on other projects and at the same time maximizes your income. Every fee structure that works should be equitable and fair to both you and your clients. You don't want to overcharge and you don't want to be taken advantage of.

Rule Don't lose work because of the rate you are charging. It is easy to have a sense of entitlement and an overinflated sense of self-worth. Consulting companies charge their developers out at $175 an hour or more, so why shouldn't you be able to charge the same amount? There are many differences in your case. Most important, your overhead should be virtually nothing if you have structured your company properly. Second, you do not need to charge a high hourly rate to make far more than $175 an hour. In all projects, plan to engage at a reasonable rate that makes you competitive (or cheaper) than lesser candidates. The difference is that you can engage on multiple projects and charge flat fees commensurate with your experience. Charging $175 an hour will price you out of most projects. Charging a flat-fee rate of $2,400 a week to engage with three clients simultaneously in a retainer-based manner (or a fixed hourly model), without having to work more hours, ensures you are very competitively priced. Even junior independent contractors who are inferior in terms of skills, communication, and presentation may charge more than you do, but they cannot deliver what you can deliver.

Hourly Fees

Hourly billing is the most common approach to billing used in the technical and professional industries. It is also the least flexible and the one that lends itself to unethical patterns of execution. For example, the more proficient you become at a specific task (programming language, architecture, deployment model, and so on) the less time it takes for you to do it, and the better the final solution is. Therefore, the client pays more for the junior developer to deliver an inferior product than they do for the senior developer to deliver a better product. You are penalized for being proficient and having expertise. Your client is penalized for working with junior level people. There is never a scenario where all parties win in traditional hourly billing.

Rule When subcontracting through consulting organizations and staffing firms, you most likely will have to bill hourly. When you do direct client work, strive to put a different model into place—either fixed hourly, fixed fee, or retainer. Hourly work should always be your last option.

Time is the common ingredient for all of us; a day holds the same number of hours for the person of poverty as the person of wealth. Two people can sit at their computers for 10 hours a day. The first can make a set portion of his salary that equates to a few hundred dollars; the second can make the same as 10 people and is limited only by the number of opportunities available.

Rule If you are going to sit behind your computer for ten hours in a day, you should work to maximize the amount of income you can make during that time. One person can make $100 dollars in a day, while the next can make $1000. Your goal should be to be as productive with your time as possible, and strive to increase your income without increasing the amount of overall time spent working.

There will be occasions when your only option to engage is at an hourly rate—primarily when you are subcontracting through an organization that only does hourly billing. In most circumstances, however, you can eliminate your role in playing into this less-than-ideal model. Here are some approaches to working within the hourly model that allows you to retain your freedom and your ethics:

1. **Agree to work for a fixed number of hours per week.** The standard full-time resource equates to 40 hours a week. Before you engage on a project, state that you will work in a full-time capacity and deliver on all of the items required, whether it takes you 20 hours a week or 60 hours a week, but that you will charge for a flat 40 hours. Have confidence in yourself and your skills. A master coder can deliver a lot more quickly on things than a junior developer, and you can reap this benefit ethically by agreeing to charge for a specific number of hours, regardless of the time use spend. In some cases, you may have to work more hours; but, with experience, it is very unlikely that you will have to work longer hour because you know how to deliver. This is essentially a fixed hourly model and it, in essence, gets rid of anything that ties you to time.

Rule Much of the world operates on a time-based hourly mind-set. It is possible to reeducate clients and engage with them in other ways, but in many cases, as a developer, you are perceived as a commodity and your skills are perceived as time based. Work with people in their language, but allow yourself to remove yourself ethically and responsibly from the time-based equation. A fixed hourly engagement allows you to meet at the client's level, to engage quickly on a project, and to avoid having to reeducate clients on the virtues of other fee structures.

2. **Base the number of hours for delivery on those worked by a reasonably skilled developer.** When determining how many hours a task should take, think of what it would take a reasonably skilled developer to do the task. Something that may take a junior developer 100 hours may take a senior developer 50 hours. An expert developer may be able to do it in 10 hours. Look at the situation and discuss your approach openly with your clients and how you make your estimates. If the task takes virtually anyone else 50 hours to do, then that is the time that is most appropriate to agree on. It is fair and valuable to yours clients—they are paying a low rate for you to deliver at a senior developer level—and it is a fair rate for you, because it allows you to balance your delivery for one client versus the work you are doing for others.

3. **Agree on old-fashioned hourly billing if it will lead to greater opportunities.** In some cases, you can agree to simple hourly billing, but this should be very rare. A client who wants mentoring based on an hourly rate is cheating you; you have years of experience and are willing to teach someone else. If it takes you an hour to impart years worth of experience, should the client pay only $100? Although inappropriate in most cases, you may have a client with whom you want to work that won't sign you on to the project any other way. Perhaps they have technology that you want to work with, or perhaps there is an opportunity for a broader project later down the road that lends itself to a higher value proposition. Be open to the idea of the hour-for-hour delivery model, but use it rarely. In most cases, clients who are not able to engage with you from the start in a "win–win," mutually equitable scenario will milk you for your value and never have any substantial work for you in the future.

CASE STUDY

One of the products with which I work extensively—15 years now—is BizTalk Server. I have a level of expertise with it that only a handful of other individuals have. What originally took me four months to build when I was new to the product now takes fraction of that. With an hourly billing model, what I would have charged originally for four months as a novice to the platform I would now only be able to charge four hours for as an expert. No matter what price I put on the hourly rate, I would still be punished for my expertise. At $100 an hour, the client would pay me $400 for what they would pay a novice programmer thousands of dollars for. The hourly model is not viable for the expert. It does not bring into account the years of experience or the vast amount of preexisting code or knowledge that can be brought to the table. For the expert coder, the only appropriate approaches are the fixed-fee model (which can be based on a fixed number of hours) or the retainer model. These models can be subjective, based on many parameters, and can be a great benefit to both you and your clients.

Fixed Fees

The ability to look at a piece of work and at a situation and know what is a fair price for it is an art, and one that comes with a great deal of experience. When the client knows exactly what a project will cost, and you know exactly what the effort required will be and what the financial gain will be, the project and the relationship can be very stress free and easy to sustain.

Professional services firms often stay away from fixed-fee engagements because the level of risk is high and the resources that may end up working on the project are unknown. A company of 500 people will end up staffing a project with resources based on when the project sells. The resources available may not be able to deliver in the same time frame or at the same level of effort as the people who put together the fixed price in the first place. But, you are not a generic professional services firm, and you most likely will be either the sole resource or a primary resource on the project you are selling.

Given that you will be engaged personally on the project, and you have done projects that are virtually the same in scope and delivery as the one in front of you, you should be very comfortable giving a fixed-fee price without having to labor too much over the specific price. If you can't see a fair price to charge immediately, chances are the project isn't a good fit for a fixed fee.

■ **Rule** The ability to state a fixed price comes from experience, with similar experiences behind you. If a fixed price doesn't immediately come to mind while you are talking with a client, chances are you should not engage in a fixed-fee pricing model. If you have to labor over the price—do analysis, get more scope, and so on—then you are better off looking at an alternative approach to pricing.

Retainer-Based Fees

The ideal situation is to engage with clients using a retainer-based model. This strategy allows for a long-term relationship—one in which your coding and your consulting can take place, and the betterment of the client is not based on hours or time, but on your skill and expertise. Retainers allow for you to engage in any capacity needed, don't require much detail for the scope of work, and create a level of trust with the client. They are also often very affordable, especially when compared with the full-time hourly model, and can be an easy sell when you are working with executive- or director-level buyers.

In general, retainers are a bargain for the client, and are great for you as long as they are in place long enough to account for the initial ramp-up and delivery on a project. You don't want to have a retainer that lasts for one or two months, because the level of work you do at the beginning of a project is usually much greater than that six months into a project. A retainer means a fixed amount of income for your presence. Some months you will work much harder than other months. A retainer works for both you and the buyer when it is a minimum of three months in duration, and, ideally, is six months in duration. This gives plenty of time to equalize the level of effort and to gain trust on both sides (your client of you and you of your client) that hopefully leads to work in the future.

There are several aspects to setting up a successful retainer-based agreement:

1. **Recurring monthly fee**. A monthly fee should be the focus of the process. A six-month, $5,000-a-month retainer is much more palatable to a buyer than a $35,000 project that ends in six months. And $5,000 a month is less than an employee would cost and is a sum virtually unheard of in professional services. It is a rate that allows you to put a lot of value into the deliverables for the client, and it allows you to engage in a variety of ways— delivery, consulting, business building, and so on.

Tip   Low monthly retainers are easy to sell because they are good for both the client and for you. If both of you see value in a price, then the price is right and the project will move forward easily. Whether the monthly fee is $5,000, $7,500, or $12,500, it is based specifically on what you will do during the process. The final price should be based on how long you can sustain the price with the client, not on short-term gain. A three-year, $5,000-a-month project is worth substantially more than a three-month, $12,500-a-month project.

---

2. **Team-based approach**. With your growth and success, more people will eventually join your team—either as contractors or as employees. Chapter 11 focuses on this growth potential, but what is important to state here is that bringing a team of people to deliver on a project can lower everyone's time commitment and improve the deliverable to the client substantially. For instance, if you have three people who all have skills that can aid in the

delivery on a project, you can engage as a single full-time resource (equating to what a single senior person could do in a 40-hour week), with each of you doing those aspects of the project that are most in line with your skills. Perhaps one of you can pound out documentation faster than another, whereas another team member can code the back-end database components, and the third is more adept at building the user interface. The client gets the best talent for each of the tasks, your team gets to deliver in a time-effective manner, and you can sell the overall project at a higher recurring rate than if there was only a single resource involved. Selling a team of people at a full-time equivalent rate of $16,500 a month, for example, is a cut rate compared with what the client would get anywhere else, and it is a great rate for you as one of many projects you are delivering on at any given time.

3. **Scope setting.** Don't focus too much on scope. Whatever you do should be above and beyond what any other resource would do, because you are operating with expert-level skills and experience. You must be confident that you can do terrific work for your client, and the easiest thing to say is, "I will deliver great work for you throughout this process. If at any time you feel that I am [or we are, if you are delivering as a team] underperforming, please call me immediately so the situation can be addressed." The goal is to make your engagement very flexible and very valuable to the client and to you. The scope should never be for specific deliverables in a certain amount of time. Think of the retainer relationship in a similar way as an employee; an employee is there to assist in a variety of things, but rarely has a specific set of deliverables due in a certain time frame. As a retainer-based contractor, you are an extension of this model—a highly effective, long-term resource that can be used in a variety of ways to better the client's condition.

Determine Appropriate Fees

Realize that you can engage profitably at virtually any price point. If you allow yourself to only work on a single project at a time, then the goal is to figure out how to charge the most for your services. If, on the other hand, your model is to engage on as many opportunities as come through your door, then the price you charge is largely irrelevant. You can focus on bringing value to clients, sharing your expertise, improving your skills, and doing quality delivery.

You set up your business to charge less than virtually anyone else, and make more than virtually anyone else. The key to doing this is to have an expansive pipeline, open communication with clients, and a mastery of skills in the technologies with which you work. Your model is to work on many projects at great rates for both you and your clients.

How do you come up with the appropriate rate to charge for a solution? There are several options:

1. **Go with experience and confidence.** Sometimes when you are presented with a solution, you know immediately what you would be willing to do the work for. When you are in a phone conversation with a client, being able to state a "ballpark figure" goes a long way in selling a project. Because you are running your company, you don't need to be secretive or slow in stating the price, and you don't need to hide behind a proposal and e-mail to give a number. Being able to state confidently the price for an engagement while actively talking with the client often allows for the verbal "go-ahead" on a project. It also allows you to work through any concerns or alterations to scope within minutes, rather than going through a lengthy paperwork process that consumes a lot of your time and that creates a lesser chance of signing on the project.

2. **Let the client have input.** Let your clients have a say in what they would be willing to pay for the work being done. You will find that people are very uncomfortable talking about money, and asking the simple question "What is your budget?" causes silence on the other end of the line. Remember that 99% of the people you come into contact with are not comfortable with money, and clients are no exception. It is your job to be confident with the topic of money and to put other people at ease. Your goal is neither to take advantage of anyone nor to steal their funds for yourself. Make them aware of this and help them to understand that both of you are parties in trying to determine the most appropriate price for a project. If you have a buyer who is open to dialog, then you can usually come up with a price that is a win for both of you. The client will be able to work with you at a rate he or she couldn't get from anyone else, and you will be able to define a scope for this rate that allows you to deliver a high-quality solution without extreme overuse of your time.

3. **Charge based on what others are charging**. Consider the following. You know that the going price for your services is $150 an hour through a consulting firm. You know that independent contractors are charging $75 an hour for the same work. You know that you can deliver a solution for a fraction of what someone else could, and deliver a higher quality product. You know that you can develop and unit test it in less than four weeks. You can say to the client, "This will cost you $10,000. I will deliver it in four weeks." Help them do the math, showing that your effective hourly bill rate is substantially lower than any of their other options. This is a win for them and a win for you; it gives everyone a great price and allows you to engage on this and other work throughout the duration of the project.

■ **Rule**   You will have more success selling smaller projects than larger projects. Selling a $10,000 project is generally quick and easy. The buyer often doesn't need to seek upper management approval because the fee is low, and it is easier for you to contain scope within a smaller price point. In some cases, larger projects will present themselves, but in general, trying to sell larger single projects requires a large amount of time from you, onsite visits, scoping documentation, and so on. Trying to sell single $120,000-project is astronomically more time-intensive than selling a $10,000-a-month recurring project that lasts for a year.

Define Your Goals for Income

Although Chapter 10 details the importance of goal setting, and provides steps you can take to make things happen that you want to see happen, it is important here to emphasize the need to state clearly your goals for income. Everyone wants to "make more money," but very few of us state specifically what this looks like. A business requires goals, and the easiest way to state goals is in financial terms.

One of the purposes of most for-profit businesses is to make money. Large businesses expend great efforts in determining financial goals for upcoming quarters and years based on previous profits, acquisitions, and market research. You, as the head of a small business—either as a solo practitioner or as the head of a very small group of people doing delivery work—can cut out the time expenditure and the paperwork, and simply sit down and state what your financial goals are. "Next year, I will make $1 million in revenue." That is all it takes to get things in motion. You must repeat that, make it real, write it down, post it in front of you, carry it around. That is your financial goal, your way of validating that what you are doing has value in the world, and that you are growing toward what you are after.

■ **Rule** Your goals should be based on nothing except for what you expect for yourself. A coder can make $60K a year or $1 million a year; there is nothing out there that limits you except for yourself and the opportunities you are able to draw to yourself. You may not be able to reach your goals tomorrow, but if you state your goals clearly and focus on them as a top priority, you will make them happen. The easiest goals to attain are those of a material nature, and money is the base of materialism. Say your goal, write it down, focus on it. It will happen if you believe it and are willing to do the work to get there.

Conclusion

Your ability to make an excellent income depends first on your mind-set. View the ability to make money in a positive light; don't look negatively at those who choose a life of wealth over a life of poverty. Next, be willing to work hard and assess everything you do; reinvent yourself and your offerings as time and the market require. Be in the habit of saying yes to every opportunity that comes your way, and never allow yourself to be in a situation in which you cannot take on additional work. Make your fees fair to your clients and to yourself; make money by assisting as many people as possible at reasonable, competitive rates. Last, make a firm statement about what you want to attain and what your financial goals are; this is critical to your ability to measure your progress and make your fortune.

Goal Setting

The Engine Behind Your Success

There is no beginning so mean, which continued application will not make considerable, and…will make it at last irresistible.

—From *Plutarch's Lives*

You are in a unique position as an independent coder and businessperson to set goals that can directly impact both your private life and professional life. If you were an employee of a large company, setting goals for the company would have no direct impact on your personal life, and setting goals in your private life would have little impact on your day-to-day success within your organization. In your case, however, the line between your professional and personal life is nonexistent. Every goal you set for yourself will potentially impact all aspects of your life, business or personal, public or private.

One of the most exciting aspects of working for yourself in an industry in which you can work from anywhere and make a significant amount of money is the fact that you have the ability to set and achieve virtually any goal. Some may require more intense determination and labor than others, but you have the freedom to aim toward just about any outcome. If you want to move to a different state, live in a foreign country, take an extended working vacation, support a charitable organization, invest in a business, spend more time with family, or change the type of project work you engage on, you can; there is nothing holding you back, and all of it can happen within the scope of your business. This level of freedom is not something most people have. To take advantage of this freedom, you need to master the art of setting and attaining goals.

Types of Goals

There are numerous types of goals that you can set for yourself. Material goals are the easiest to attain, while those that are nonmaterial (or idealistic) are the most difficult. If your only goals in life are material, you will likely succeed in attaining them, but you will never be satisfied with what you have gained. The passion for material gain knows no bounds, and must be tempered by interests and goals that are aligned with ideals and actions that have no direct monetary or material value. "It is difficult, if not impossible," writes Schopenhauer in *The Wisdom of Life*, "to define the limits which reason should impose on the desire for wealth; for there is no absolute or definite amount of wealth which will satisfy a man. Riches, one may say, are like sea-water: the more you drink, the thirstier you become."

There is nothing inherently wrong with setting financial goals, but you should have nonmaterial goals that underlie your desire to increase your capital. For example, if your goal is $1 million of annual income, is it to allow you to increase your possessions, or is it to free you up to pursue other interests and to make the world, as you see it, a better place? Pursuing money for the sake of making more money is avarice, while pursuing money for the sake of increasing your ability to make an impact on the world is altruism. Both lead to an increase in funds; the only difference between the two is the intent behind the action. One leads to harm, the other to good.

Chapter 12 outlines how to think about and use the money that your business generates. For now, as you think about goal setting, realize that you need to include goals both for your business and for your personal life. For purposes of this discussion, business goals will be mainly financial in nature (building your business to enable you to make more profit and increase profit for others that work with you), while personal goals will be primarily idealistic in nature (pursuing those goals that allow you to improve and alter the world).

Rule   The end result of your code-focused business should be the funding of the idealistic focuses of your personal endeavors. There are certainly many businesses that cross over from purely materialistic (or "for profit") in nature to highly idealistic (either "partially for profit" or "not for profit"). If you want to engage in a business that is not focused entirely on the generation of capital, then it should be separate from your coding or services business. Your work is meant to enable others to build their businesses, and you are working within a corporate framework. Keep your business goals primarily materialistic in nature, and your personal goals focused on what is truly important in this life.

Business Goals

Your business goals are specific to the health, growth, and profit of your business transactions. However, every choice you make in your business should ultimately be made to support personal goals that you have. You are in business by yourself, and you are not an employee. You are in business to support your ultimate personal goals of wealth and independence, and therefore you are in a unique position to base every business decision you make on its impact on your personal life. Think of your business as a dynamic entity that you can mold to ensure you are always getting closer to your personal goals. When making goals for your business, consider the following questions:

1. **Does this business goal support my personal values and vision?** In everything that you do, ensure that you are engaging in an ethical way that supports how you would want to see things done in the world. The pursuit of money has caused many people to do things against their conscience. Don't be one of them. You have ultimate freedom in how you engage, so always choose the high road that supports your understanding, your values, and your vision.

2. **Will this business goal help me to attain my personal goals?** Your personal goals outweigh all other aspects of your business. If what you are doing is not getting you closer to your personal goals, then you need to redirect your energies immediately. If you are working on a job that pays marginally and requires you to be away from home every week, but your goal is to spend time with your family, then you need to change immediately. You have the ability to transform your business to support you in whatever goals you are after, and that is the sole purpose for engaging in an independent business.

3. **Is what I am doing a good use of my time?** There is a limited amount of time in your day, and the work that you do needs to be valuable. Ideally, you are making significant profit, and can see the value in your labor. If you are not making high wages, or the work is taking you away from other things that you see more value in, then you need to rethink what you are doing. If you don't believe in the value of what you are doing, you won't be able to attain the end goals that you are after.

4. **Are the people working with me being well uti-lized and improving their lot?** Everyone who works with you (subcontractors, employees, and partners) should be better off working with you, and see the ben-efit (financially and otherwise) of doing work with you. If anyone has negative feelings toward you, or feels that they are putting in more than they are getting out, the relationship needs to be either repaired or terminated. Often, people who work for you will have their own challenges in life, and their upset or anger will manifest toward those they believe have control over what they are doing. As an employer, even in a disconnected and independent manner, you will become the target for their upset and anger. Negativity coming from anyone on your team (including you) will adversely affect your ability to achieve your goals.

5. **Are the businesses that I work for better off with me involved?** If you are improving clients' situations and are a valuable asset, you will create an energy that leads to more success. If you are an impediment or a detriment to a client project (through either lack of skills or poor attitude), then you will create an energy that detracts from your ability to attain your goals.

6. **Am I enjoying the overall process and scope of work that I am engaged in?** Individual projects or clients may, considered alone, be uninteresting or difficult, but as a whole, is the business that you are engaged in challenging, interesting, and rewarding? If not, then your attitude will be impacted negatively, and your ability to achieve your goals will be hindered.

Notice that none of these goals are specific to the business itself. All of them are about either your personal life or the enrichment of those around you. Your business should be viewed as a means to an end. It exists for the improvement of you and the client. It is not a corporation that exists to increase profits for shareholders and expand operations indefinitely. It exists as an extension of yourself, and allows you to take the path to wealth and independence. Every goal you make in business should further your personal advancement or the improvement of those who you work with.

Personal Goals

In order for your business to prosper, you have to set personal goals. Personal goals should range from simple material goals of lifestyle and income to complex, idealistic goals that allow your vision to become a reality in the larger world. All of your focus should not be on the growth of your business or on the attainment of money. If you are at your core someone who dreams of growing and running a company, independence is not in your nature, and the rules in this book do not apply well to you. The assumption is that you are someone who wants to use your business as a vehicle to attain personal wealth and independence in order to pursue those things in life that are outside of the scope of commerce and services.

A person who seeks wealth and independence is someone who should have broad vision on how these will be used once achieved. Your personal goals need to be large, visionary, and tailored to your interests and the betterment of your world. Take the following into consideration when making personal goals:

1. **Will my financial goals ultimately get me closer to independence, or will they lock me down and tie me to material possessions?** A rule of economics is that the more you make, the more you need to make. Many people who live in multimillion-dollar homes can barely afford their mortgages. People who are extremely wealthy one year file for bankruptcy the next. You need to make sure that as you make more money, you don't fall into a pattern of requiring more income just to satisfy your lifestyle. If you want to make $1 million in a year, will that require that you make $2 million the next year to satisfy your material acquisitions?

2. **Will achieving my goals allow me to pursue what truly interests me?** Many people have difficulty defining what they want out of life. Most go along, asleep, with whatever happens, never waking to realize their purpose or create their destiny. Are your goals and ambitions getting you closer to your interests and true purpose? There must be meaning behind your goals, or they are virtually worthless to set.

3. **Do my goals focus solely on the material world of acquisition, or do they allow me to focus on idealistic (spiritual/philanthropic/humanitarian) goals as well?** As previously stated, do not pursue money solely for the attainment of that money. There must be a useful purpose behind the acquisition of capital, or you will stand a good chance of losing what you have gained.

4. **Will I be able to give more to the world and those around me as I get closer to my goals?** Your goals should broaden your ability to impact the world. With increased resources comes increased responsibility. If you don't want to have an impact on your world, or more responsibilities in your life, then you should not be pursuing wealth and independence.

5. **Are my goals going to take me away from the things that are most important to me?** Make sure you prioritize your goals. Making a million dollars in a year and spending large amounts of time with your children are not mutually exclusive. You can do both, but you must determine which is of higher priority. Your idealistic pursuits (time with children) should always take precedence over your material pursuits (make more money). You can succeed with both as long as your priorities are correct.

When you execute on goals in your private life, you will find that your business supports you. New opportunities will appear when they are needed that would not have appeared had you not taken steps to proceed with your goals in private life. The broader your vision, and the higher you set your expectations with your goals, the more your business will increase to support you. Make sure everything is in alignment, that you have prioritized properly, and that your vision and values are supported, and then be prepared as things materialize around you to support the achievement of your goals.

How to Define and Execute on Goals

Determining what your goals are can be a very challenging activity. The concept of identifying goals seems easy enough, but the reality of stating specifically what you want is difficult...so difficult, that most people never do it. Being able to state exactly what you want and then envision how to get there is what separates those who have a measure of control over their lives from those who simply float through life. All of the individuals who have accomplished great things had specific goals that they set out to achieve, and were willing to do the work required to attain them. If you want greatness in your life, you must learn to define your goals and execute on attaining them. The following list outlines the steps necessary to do this:

1. **Use a pen and paper**. Leave your computer behind. Take a pen and paper and head somewhere away from distractions. You don't want any external influence on you when you are brainstorming about your goals. You certainly don't want to be checking your e-mail or responding to texts; leave you cell phone at home. Be alone with your thoughts and focus on what it is you want to do with your life, and what that means for your business aspirations. Remember that your life goals will influence the success of your business. Small dreams will result in small results. Think big, and write down everything. Figure 10-1 shows an example of high-level, short-term, business goals; a few notes stuck to the desk that can be referenced continually and revised as needed is the ideal approach to writing up your goals.

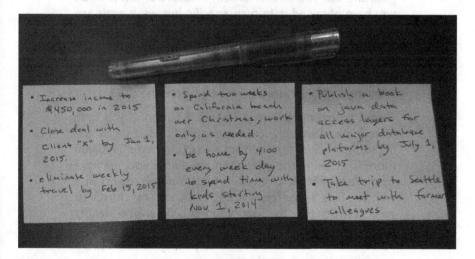

Figure 10-1. Keep your goal lists simple and fluid, easy to review and revise

Rule Always write down your goals. There is a great deal of power in the act of writing down what you want. Thinking is powerful, but translating thought to words helps solidify and make goals concrete. Some goals are extremely abstract, and writing them down clearly and concisely can take time and persistence. If you can't write down your goal, then it is unlikely that you can truly identify what it is that you want, much less attain it.

2. **Be specific.** Generalizations are simple, but of little value. "I want to be rich" or "I want to be more successful" are broad statements that cannot easily be executed on. You must state exactly what you want. "I want to make $400,000 more in revenue this year than I did last year" is a valid, actionable goal, while "I want to make a lot of money this year" is of no use to you. The former is a specific goal, one that you can measure whether you are getting closer to achieving, while the latter is a nebulous goal, one that you cannot directly measure or know when you have obtained it. In turn, specific but weak goals are easily attained but won't get you to where you really want to be, while specific and strong goals will. The difference between making your goal "climb a mountain" versus "climb Mt. Everest" is immense, and the path to attaining each is drastically different from the other.

3. **Begin to execute immediately.** As soon as you have identified and written down your specific goals, begin taking steps to achieve them. If your goal is to make $400,000 more in revenue this year, then you know you will have to make significant changes in your business. Invest in a website, hire a mentor, write a book, and reach out to your network to create opportunities. When you identify a goal, you will have a variety of ideas about how you can achieve it. As these ideas come to you, write them down and follow through on them.

Rule The moment you have determined that a goal is worth pursuing, you must begin executing on steps that you know are required for you to reach your goal. If you wait, the initial energy created with the identification of the goal will dissipate, and the likelihood of accomplishing the goal will diminish.

4. **Constantly keep your goals in mind.** Constantly think about and assess progress on the goals you have set for yourself. You must always be focused on a goal to make it happen. People who are goal driven know what they are after, and always have it in their consciousness. You are not serious about your goals unless you are working to attain them in everything that you do. If your goals are worth attaining, focus on them at all times.

■ **Rule**   We become that which we think. If your mind is focused on positive goals, you'll end up attaining them. If your mind is focused on irrelevancies or negativity, you'll end up reflecting that in your life.

---

5. **Review progress.** Periodically review what you have written down, and see how you have progressed. Have you taken steps to achieve your goals? If you are noticing no progress, then you can reassess; either the goal is not realistic or you don't have true interest in achieving it, in either of which case you need to remove it. If you see progress, note it. Perhaps you can speed up progress, or perhaps you can further define it in order to more easily attain it.

6. **Refine and expand.** As you make progress, you will be able to give more detail on the specifics of what you are trying to attain. The original goal of making $400,000 additional revenue in a year becomes, "Work with more subcontractors, expand business within current client base, engage in nine-month project with professional mentor," all of which in turn create more goals. The more you come back to your goal list and refine it, the more time you are spending thinking about what you truly want and how you can achieve it.

```
┌─────────────────────────────────────────────────────────────────┐
│                         CASE STUDY                                │
└─────────────────────────────────────────────────────────────────┘
```

In my early thirties, as I was out for a walk one evening, I made a financial goal of earning $1 million in revenue in a single year. I also set a goal that I would no longer travel at some point. I told myself that I would achieve both of these goals within three years. At the time, I was making a fraction of that income and traveling to client sites every week as an independent contractor. After the walk, in the same evening, I submitted an idea for a book to a publisher. The same week, I set up an LLC through which I would do all of my business moving forward. By the end of the year, my book was published, and I gained a number of new clients. By the end of the following year, I was traveling for only a few days a month and had a handful of additional clients, all of whom I was able to work for remotely. In three years, a number of subcontractors had joined my team, and I had attained my financial goal.

Throughout this process, I had maintained a focus on these two business goals, realizing both would have significant impacts on both my professional life and my private life. These goals were my primary focus, and I thought about them daily. Had I not set these specific goals and solidified them in my mind (and on paper), I would not have acted quickly or decisively enough to create the opportunities that allowed me to achieve these results.

Setting Realistic Goals

Set your goals high enough that they are unattainable to you today but within reason of what is possible for you to achieve in the short and long term. Realistic goals can still be lofty, but they must be concrete, and you must have some ideas for actionable steps that you can take to achieve your goals.

To illustrate, imagine a scenario in which you are a developer who has a deep background in .NET and SQL, and basic exposure to several Microsoft platforms (such as SharePoint). You are currently making $200,000 a year working as a subcontractor. You travel on a weekly basis to be onsite with clients. You need to answer three primary questions in order to set realistic goals. First, is there enough of a demand for your skillset that you can find work? Second, what is the top-level income for the kind of work you do? Third, what are acceptable travel conditions?

Beginning with skills, it is obvious that you need additional skills. Deep skills in .NET and SQL are valuable, but you will have a very difficult time finding a high volume of work to keep you steadily employed, let alone enough to keep you busy on multiple projects (a requirement for high levels of pay, as outlined in Chapter 9). You need to supplement your skillset with expertise in one or more platforms (for example, leverage the basic skills in SharePoint into mastery of an aspect of the product).

A high-level goal in this scenario would be to "Get on a SharePoint-specific project to gain expertise with the product, and focus on custom .NET components within SharePoint to utilize current skills." This goal can be broken down into two very achievable goals, such as "Call key people in my network and see if I can engage on a SharePoint project for a discounted price in order to begin immediately," and "Invest immediately in SharePoint training."

Moving on to finances, you need to determine what a realistic income can be for someone at your level in your profession, and determine how to increase your income accordingly. Financial goals are some of the easiest to execute on and attain, because you have a direct measure of success. Set your expectations high, and put a timeline on them. As an independent coder, you should be able to make $250,000 a year with ease in a remote, nontraveling capacity. You should be able to make $500,000 a year if you are doing intelligent advertising, keeping your network healthy and active, and saying yes to everything that comes along. It is possible to make more than $500,000 a year, but you have to make achieving that goal your primary concern and be willing to put in the time and thought.

If you are making $200,000 a year currently, then a goal of "I will make $250,000 this year, and $400,000 next year" is completely within reach. Once you have this goal in mind, though, you next need to break it into smaller goals that will lead to reaching those numbers, such as, "I will publish a book within the next eight months," "I will purchase appropriate insurance so that I can engage on healthcare projects," and "I will take a trip to Denver to meet with my former colleagues and clients in order to try and create some new opportunities."

Last, you need to address travel; namely, what level of travel is required for you to support your financial and personal needs? Chapter 1 focuses on travel and outlines why the majority of travel is nonessential. Your key goal here begins with, "I will eliminate nonessential travel." You then must supplement this top-level goal with more refined, detailed goals. One example would be, "I will tell my current client that as of January 1st, I will no longer be able to travel onsite except in rare cases. I will tell them that if they would like to continue to work with me, I can reduce my rates, or come up with a revised list of tasks. If they do not wish to work with me, I will find other clients who will allow for remote work."

As you can see, breaking high-level goals into smaller and more granular goals takes things from abstract levels down to attainable goals that you can execute on immediately. One of the primary secrets to executing successfully on goals is to ensure that you are working on something that you can start immediately. You want exciting goals ("I want to make a million dollars a year") that are made up of many smaller, atomic goals that are easy to act on ("I will invest in the services of a mentor by the end of next week" and "I will reach out to my contacts to find another project"). By doing this, you take goals that seem impossible to attain at the moment and turn them into goals that are very realistic to complete in the near term.

■ **Rule** Timelines that you place on attaining goals should be aggressive, but also based on some measure of reality. If your goal is to have a million dollar a year income but you have no published books, no clients, and no significant money that you want to invest in transforming your business overnight with the help of external experts, then it is highly unlikely that you will achieve your goals.

The Impact of Thought

You achieve goals through hard work and the basic approaches outlined in this chapter, but you also must have a solid foundation of thought that supports what you are aiming for. If you don't believe in the value of your goals, if you don't think that they are really attainable, or if you know you are not willing to do the work required, then there is no point in pretending that you have a valid goal. Goals must be backed by a deep level of commitment if you want to see them come to fruition.

When you have identified a goal, you must then see yourself as having attained that goal. In *The Power of Awareness*, Neville Goddard writes, "Perpetual construction of future states without the consciousness of already being them, that is, picturing your desire without actually assuming the feeling of the wish fulfilled, is the fallacy and mirage of mankind. It is simply futile day-dreaming."

Your actions and your persona must show that you have achieved the goal, even if you have not yet. For example, after you have been coding for several years, you can quickly pick up new languages and platforms with relative ease. If you want to truly master a platform, you need to engage on a billable project; only by using a technology can you really understand it. Therefore, if your goal is to work with a new platform, first learn the basics of it, and after you have this foundational understanding, begin promoting yourself as a developer on that technology.

To illustrate, assume that you are looking to engage on a Microsoft Dynamics AX solution. First, you work with the product in a development environment to understand the basics. Next, you tell everyone you know that you are you are looking for AX development project work. Regardless of what comes along, you take it, whether it pays well or not. You see yourself as an AX developer, others see you as an AX developer, and AX developer opportunities begin to appear. Your skills ensure that you can work with it. Your mindset says you are already a viable developer. Your goal has been identified, and you have taken steps to achieve it.

■ **Rule** You must see yourself as having already achieved your goal, whether related to your skillset, your finances, your offerings, or your personal life.

The importance of your mental attitude and activity in achieving your goals is enormous, and cannot be overemphasized. Many people say they want something, but don't do what is necessary to successfully acquire it. People who have never realized their dreams, their desires, or their ambitions are all around us. Some blame circumstances, others blame environment, but ultimately we only have ourselves to blame if we fail to achieve our goals. What you must realize is that virtually anything is possible, and within the very material world of business and services, all goals are attainable if you are willing to take the steps necessary to identify them and execute on achieving them.

CASE STUDY

I had a goal of doubling my yearly business income. I stated the exact cash value that I expected to increase my income by. I believed that I would reach this level, and had such confidence that I purchased an income-producing rental property that same week. I saw myself as having achieved the goal, and I believed that somehow things would come together to allow me to succeed in increasing my income. I was ready to do the work that I knew was necessary. By purchasing something I could not immediately afford, I was putting faith into the process of goal attainment. Many would look at this as high risk, and there is some truth to that. Achieving wealth and independence requires risk. Achieving lofty goals requires risk. But it is relative risk, and knowing that there are laws to business and accomplishing goals that, if followed, will lead to success, then the risk is only a perceived risk. Sitting in a plane at 30,000 feet would be risky if there were no laws governing aerodynamics, but with the laws established, you can be 100% certain you won't fall out of the sky as long as there are no negative factors (birds, missiles, bad engines). The same is true with the laws that govern achieving goals. As long as you can identify the goal, immediately take steps to attain that goal, and envision yourself having already reached that goal, then you will succeed with achieving whatever you have set for yourself.

Conclusion

As an independent service provider, you have the freedom to direct your course in virtually any direction you choose. The goals you set in your personal life will directly influence the success or failure of the goals you set in your professional life (and vice versa). Without goals, you have no direction. With goals, you can influence your own destiny. Material goals are generally much more easy to attain than idealistic goals, but without idealistic goals, you will likely find that your material goals will not materialize. Once you have identified your goals, you must immediately execute in order to attain them. You must also conceptualize yourself having already attained the goals, and believe in the value of what it is you are after. Through identification, execution, and the power of thought, you will succeed in achieving what you have set for yourself.

Growth and Expansion

Handling Success

The purpose of life for man is growth, just as the purpose of life for trees and plants is growth. Man is formed for growth, and he is under the necessity of growing. It is essential to his happiness that he should continuously advance.

—Wallace D. Wattles, *The Science of Being Great*

Success will come to you. You have to plan for it, and prepare for it. If you are following the path to wealth and independence, and you are investing the work and thought necessary, your income will grow and your opportunities will increase. What you originally were able to handle on your own will eventually become something that you need assistance with. You'll engage in bigger projects, with more resources representing you and your work. Your private life will expand and your dreams will grow.

This chapter begins with several discussions about preparing for your success and pushing your business to grow. It then looks at very pragmatic steps to take to work with subcontractors and employees to support and sustain your growth. Being aware of the realities of growth is important so that you can decide for yourself in what direction to take your business as you embrace new opportunities and search for ways to improve your levels of income and independence. You can control the type of growth that occurs, and can be strategic about how to harness this growth to increase your wealth while maintaining your independence.

Preparing for Financial Success

Polite society does not discuss religion or politics. Additionally, polite society does not discuss income or debts. Your success will likely catapult you out of polite society into a position where you will need to, at a minimum, discuss issues related to income and finances. If you come from a background of wealth, you may not have many concerns here, but if, like most programmers, you are self-made and do not come from money, then you will likely need to work through the process of becoming comfortable with your success. Here are some ideas on how you can prepare for financial success:

1. **Have a healthy distrust of material riches.** Never trust in your riches, and make sure you are not tied to a certain lifestyle. If you lose your money, it should only be a setback, not a disaster. For more thoughts on this, read the section "Get Comfortable with Money" in Chapter 9. Always realize the dangers inherent with money and material assets, and keep things in check as you increase your wealth.

2. **Know how you will use wealth.** Have a plan for utilizing your wealth. See Chapter 12 for a detailed discussion about this.

3. **Be prepared to be judged.** As soon as you begin to make a mark in the world, people will be there to judge you. Make sure that the things you are doing with your wealth reflect your own personal values, and that the way you use your money is based on your idealism. You will be judged regardless of what you do, so do what you think is right, and what you would hope someone in your position would do with their money.

4. **Accept that you have wealth.** Many people who are making $200,000 to $500,000 a year don't consider themselves to have much money. Because of debts and obligations, they feel that they are barely getting by. Realize the abundance that you have and that whether you are making $200K or $1 million a year, you are making substantially more than most people will ever make. Be excited about your cash flow, and realize what you have. Don't continue with a poverty mentality that you may have developed in your youth.

5. **Don't change**. Do not let wealth change you, let it enhance you. People who make their money unexpectedly are often ruined by it. The lottery winner is at much greater risk of financial collapse than is the self-made businessperson. You are at risk if you make large sums of money before you are prepared for it, or if you personally have not had a hand in creating it. Make sure that you are prepared for money, and that you do not allow it to impact who you are or what your values are.

6. **Have a value system**. Riches without a spiritual or philosophical foundation are treacherous. If you want wealth and independence, you should first have a moral and philosophical platform that will give you the strength to deal judiciously with your material riches. Without a solid base, you can easily be ruined.

Forcing Growth

Most everyone who has a business wants to see growth, and many want to see it occur on their timeline. The magic of business is that, by taking the appropriate steps with regard to advertising, skill development, networking, and solid delivery work, your business will grow and your income will increase. You do not have to take extra steps to force growth to occur on your timeline. Often, the healthiest businesses are those that allow themselves to grow naturally. This being said, you can in fact take steps to force the growth of your business.

Should you decide that you need to exert your will on your business and make it grow on a specific timeline, be aware that you will likely succeed, but there may be unanticipated consequences. Drawing an analogy to produce, all fruits and vegetables will grow on their own through sunlight, water, and proper tending. In due time, they will develop into their natural state. In our modern society, this often isn't enough, and we want to grow things on our timeline and to our dimensions. Genetically modifying food puts controls on the process and causes the produce to grow specifically to the requirements of the grower.

There is certainly controversy over what is better, the natural produce or the GM produce. The first appeals to those who embrace the natural state of things, whereas the second appeals to those who want a specific product that looks a certain way on a certain schedule and is immune to many of the diseases that attack produce in its natural state. The end result, though, with both is that there is produce that can be consumed. Is a strawberry that is small, natural in color, and somewhat flavorful better than a strawberry that is twice the size, bright red, and tasteless? It depends on the consumer.

All of this applies to your business. You can either allow your business to grow naturally, believing that if you take the proper steps you will end with a healthy product that will support your needs, or you can inject your business and force it to grow on your own terms. Exerting your will can work, but you may or may not like the outcome.

The following list outlines several approaches that will jump-start your business and lead to immediate growth. Some are very risky (or costly) financially, but you'll find that they do work. Only those who risk will acquire wealth and independence, which means you are likely open to some level of risk.

1. **Hire a mentor or business strategist.** If you want growth, work with someone who can get you to where you want to be. Your mentor needs to be someone who has attained the level of success that you want to attain. Hire their services over an extended period of time. Typically, mentors work with you over a period of 6 to 9 months minimum. During this time, they strategize with you to determine what your goals are, and work with you to attain them. Working with a qualified mentor who has attained a higher level of success than you have will open doors that you cannot open for yourself. The act of paying and engaging with a mentor will transform your business, and set you in a direction you cannot anticipate. Expect to pay a mentor on average $5,000 to $7,500 a month for a period of time. It is similar to hiring an executive-level partner for a short period of time, and can have amazing results.

2. **Spend your money.** Chapter 12 discusses at length investing in your business and those around you. In short, if you want to make money, you must be willing to spend it. Large investments, made with intention, intelligence, and strategy, can lead to massive growth. There are many independent businesspeople who refuse to invest even tiny amounts of money into their business (for example, "I am making $300,000 a year, but I can't afford to invest in a $1,500 website"). If you are willing to spend on your business, you will see your business grow.

3. **Hire an employee or a subcontractor on a retainer.** Taking on a new person can cause growth through two primary means. First, you have someone to take over portions of your project work so that you can focus on the growth of your business. Second (and more important), you create a new offering, which generates new opportunities. You can tell your clients and your leads that you

now have an additional person who brings new skills to the table (or simply another hand to work on things). Having someone new on your team creates energy and options that could not surface without their presence.

4. **Take advertising and marketing seriously**. See Chapter 6 for details about what you can do, and how best to spend your time here. Taking serious steps to implement advertising and marketing collateral will have immediate impacts on the success of your business. Plan to invest a sizeable percentage of your income to this area to get things started. Investing 15% to 20% will have massive impacts, if you are willing to take the risk to spend that much.

5. **Share your work**. If you have a lot of work, bring someone else in and the work and opportunities will increase. (This could be a subcontractor, employee, or a partner.) Share in the spirit of creating more for everyone, and never fear sharing work because of competition or the threat that you might lose the work to someone you bring in. The more you share with others, the more that will be returned to you.

6. **Visit in person as many people in your network as possible**. Take a working vacation and hit the road. Visit with every contact you can think of. Offer to take people out to lunch or dinner, and meet with them at their convenience. Meet with former clients and colleagues, warm leads, and dead opportunities. Sacrificing your time and money and prospecting for work will almost always lead to results. Take three or four weeks and use it to create new business.

7. **Donate your money**. If you want to see radical change in your business or your personal assets, donate a sizeable portion of your income. Take 10% of your earnings (pre-tax) for a specific period of time and donate it to the charity or cause of your choice. You will see results that you cannot predict, but you will have identified yourself as a conduit for resources that find their way to those in need, and the energetic force that you've created will ensure that there is more than enough to replace what you have just given so that you can give even more in the future.

Always know that, while these approaches will cause growth, the outcome may or may not be to your liking. For example, hiring an employee opens new opportunities, but you now have a dependent employee who expects a certain income. You've given up a piece of your independence to attain a specific financial outcome (though there are ways to mitigate this, as outlined in the section "Working with Employees," later in this chapter). If you let your business grow on its own, you will reach wealth and independence in due time.

Working with Subcontractors

You can subcontract on your engagements, and you can have others subcontract for you. The process and paperwork are extremely simple. The working relationships are generally highly flexible and easy to maintain. Having two or three people that you work with on a variety of projects is a better approach than working with many new people. You will develop trust and know how different people work in different scenarios. Ideally, several of the people will work with you on a nearly continual basis, and you can help each other build your respective businesses.

Subcontractor Rates and Relationships

Your subcontractors need to understand your working model, whatever it may be. In most cases, you do not need to tell a subcontractor how much money you receiving from a client for a project, or what percentage of that income the subcontractor will be earning, but you do need to make it clear that you are profiting from their work. They need to understand that your profit comes from the fact that you have sold the project and have done the work to establish the client relationship. The work wouldn't exist for your subcontractor if you were not involved in the process, and there is value in that.

■ **Rule** The rates you negotiate with your subcontractors should be based on fair terms that both of you agree to. In some cases, you will want to use an hourly rate, in others a fixed price, and in others a percentage of the total income from a project. In all cases, the rate should be based on what is fair between you and your subcontractor, and not based directly on the income you are getting from your client.

The various models that you can use for client engagements are outlined in Chapter 9: hourly, retainer, and fixed fee. For hourly projects, you may pay your subcontractor a percentage of that hourly fee. For a retainer or fixed-fee project, you may pay your subcontractor hourly, with the expectation that the number of hours they put in will be substantially lower than the value of your retainer. Figure out a model that is of value to your subcontractor and allows you to make a profit. There is certainly a way to structure any arrangement so that both of you feel like you are getting a great deal.

You will have an abundance of work as you progress, and you should let your team of subcontractors know that as long as they want work, you can provide it, but they need to be creative in their pricing strategies with you, just like you are with your clients. Let them know that if they stipulate a flat rate of $65 an hour regardless of the project, you will have only sporadic work for them, whereas if they are always willing to be flexible in their billing rates, you will have a continuous stream of work for them that will ultimately be worth far more than $65 an hour. It is easier to sell multiple lower-paying jobs that together net far more than a single high-paying job, and your subcontractors need to understand your model.

Your subcontractors need to have the same mindset as you: highly independent and flexible, and willing to go where the market leads. The more open you are with the people you work with, the more likelihood they will be able to help you sustain and grow your business while working to grow their own.

Subcontractor Paperwork

A subcontractor differs from an employee in several ways. The IRS defines who it considers to be a subcontractor vs. an employee for tax purposes. According to the IRS, the two most important characteristics that differentiate a subcontractor from an employee are that the subcontractor works with their own tools and equipment, aren't controlled by you in where they work, and they make less than 70% of their yearly income from any one business. Unless you want to run the risk of having the IRS designate a subcontractor as an employee of yours, with the associated tax burden that carries, do not provide equipment and tools to contractors, make sure they have an independent place of business established, and mandate that they make at least 30% of their yearly income from other clients (which you can assist with by connecting them with jobs you are not interested in). Make sure that you are supporting subcontractors in their independence and that you are meeting the legal requirements defined by the IRS to avoid having the subcontractors considered employees.

In addition to ensuring that subcontractors meet the preceding requirements, you must have several documents in place when working with subcontractors, as follows:

1. **Contract.** This is a basic contract outlining the services being performed and the fees being paid. This contract will look identical in structure to the contracts that you have put together for your clients, as outlined in detail in Chapter 8. In the case of a subcontractor, you are the client and they are the vendor; either one of you can create the contract, but you need something on file for each project to meet IRS requirements.

2. **W-9.** A W-9 is a Request for Taxpayer Identification Number (TIN) or Certification. It supplies you (the client) with the subcontractor's mailing address and TIN, which you will use at the end of the year to send out 1099-MISC tax forms. This ensures that every dollar you spend on subcontractors is accounted for with the IRS, and that you can expense all of it through your business.

3. **1099-MISC.** This is a form that you fill out at the end of the year for every subcontractor, which notes how much you paid them and what their TIN is. You send a copy to the IRS, send a copy to the subcontractor, and keep a couple of copies for yourself for your own tax paperwork.

If you have a small group of subcontractors that you work with on a regular basis, and they have skills that allow you to sell in a broad range of industries, you'll be well supported as you continue to pursue your own business successes.

Working with Employees

There is only one reason you should ever hire an employee: the project work you are selling requires that you do so. If you do hire an employee, you must make the arrangement such that they are paid only if they engage in billable work. If you agree to pay a guaranteed salary to someone, you have created dependency and expectation, and have strayed from the path of independence that is one of your most basic goals. For you, as an independent developer and businessperson, hiring an employee should be purely for insurance and contractual requirements with clients, and you should never guarantee an employee a recurring income.

Rule   You are pursuing independence through your business. Hiring an employee means a level of dependence that you should incur only in rare circumstances; otherwise, you run the risk of losing your independence.

CASE STUDY

I do a lot of work within healthcare. The industry is heavily regulated, and the rules of engagement are constantly changing. The Health Insurance Portability and Accountability Act (HIPAA) compliance rules govern the prerequisites for businesses to work with protected health information (PHI). PHI includes patient records and personal information. The HIPAA regulations state, in part, that any individual who is going to work with PHI data must comply with several rules, one of which is to carry a certain level of insurance. This insurance covers liability in the case of breach of data (a laptop with PHI on it gets stolen, for example), which can result in significant financial fines from the federal government. The insurance must be carried by any vendor that wants to do business involving PHI. In addition to obtaining the insurance, a number of contracts (business-associated agreements, or BAAs) must be signed.

In most of my healthcare solutions, the projects require that I engage other resources in addition to myself. I generally work with one or two other people on my team to share load and ensure someone is always available to answer a call or work on a solution. The people on my team have two choices. Their first choice is to work with me in the preferred role of subcontractor (1099, corporation to corporation). If they do this, then they must carry all of the insurance and also sign all of the special contracts required by the client and by the government. The insurance costs are high and the policies are time-consuming to validate and put into place, but it is possible to do. However, the contractual piece of getting the client to sign on with multiple individual parties is not easy, and in many cases would derail the project (for example, the client wants to work with a team, and does not want to sign individual agreements with many loosely connected developers).

Their second choice is to become an employee of my company, which has the insurance and contracts already in place. This allows everyone to easily and legally engage in project work, and presents a unified team to the client.

Because of these insurance and paperwork requirements, I requested the group of subcontractors I traditionally work to convert to employee status, and they agreed. The financial gains of working in a way that is easy and legal for healthcare clients outweighed the negatives of hiring (and being) an employee.

In some cases, work will necessitate that you hire employees. But do it with caution, and only when required. I waited many years before I swapped to using employees, and if it were not for the healthcare regulations, I would swap everyone back to subcontractor status immediately.

Paying Employee Taxes

When you work with subcontractors, everyone is responsible for their own taxes. Your client pays you, you pay your subcontractors as a simple expense, and your subcontractors figure out their own tax burden. When you hire employees, however, you are responsible for paying the taxes; this is known as withholding. Consequently, you should pay employees less money than subcontractors, because the taxes are higher for you as an employer.

As an independent contractor, you are taxed what is called self-employment tax, which includes Social Security and Medicare taxes, and has a rate of around 13%. On every $100 you make, you have to pay $13 in self-employment taxes. If you were an employee, this burden would be decreased by over half, as your employer would have to pay the other half for you. The simple way to look at this as an employer is that you will pay an additional 6.5% in Social Security/Medicare taxes for an employee. This means that if you pay both an employee and a subcontractor $50 an hour, you actually pay the subcontractor $50 an hour but pay the employee $50 + 6.5%, which would be $53.25 an hour.

Additionally, you have to pay payroll taxes, which vary between localities and states. Payroll taxes include workers' compensation taxes and applicable local taxes. Because these taxes vary by locale, you'll need to consult a CPA to find out exactly what the costs will be to you, but you can figure that an employee will cost you a minimum of 9% more than a subcontractor in taxes alone. If you were to pay benefits, that would cost even more (never pay benefits to yourself or to other employees through your business; make yours a personal expense).

CASE STUDY

My business is located in Colorado, and everyone who engages with me as an employee is also based in the state. I have a very easy relationship with these individuals, and we have known and worked with each other for years. I told them that if they wanted to work on healthcare projects, they would have to swap to employee status. I informed them that I would calculate their fee on a monthly basis based on the amount of work that I billed for their service, and then I would reduce it by 9% to cover the costs associated with paying taxes for them. They agreed, and they make almost the same rate as they would as subcontractors, and my costs are covered by the 9% reduction in rate. This 9% is based on costs specific to where I am in Colorado, and will vary in other locations.

Employee Rates and Relationships

You can use the simple formula of deducting the ~9% in employee tax costs from any rate that you pay, but first you need to determine what the fair rate is. Determine the rate much the same way as outlined earlier for subcontractors (see "Subcontractor Rates and Relationships"). You need to have an open dialogue with employees about the way you do business, and make it clear that you will be making a profit from the relationship. You should also make it clear that you are paying the employees based on income that they produce, and not on a specific salary. Their pay will increase and diminish based on workload, and you are not responsible for a set payment. They can continue to work with other companies. They are employees in paperwork only, and need to understand that you are neither going to act as a traditional boss nor guarantee their income. You must remain independent even as you bring on employees.

Figure 11-1 is a simple illustration showing that your income stays static, while that of your employees and contractors varies by month. Each month you will have different work for them to engage in, and you are not guaranteeing that they will get a specific amount of money. You are taking on as little risk as possible in order to ensure that all of you can engage on any type of project that comes along.

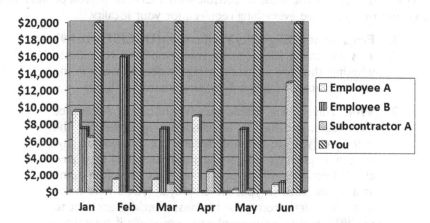

Figure 11-1. Employees and subcontractors have variable incomes; you have steady income

---

■ **Rule** Do not hire employees with salary or benefits. Make their income dependent on their billable work, and treat them like subcontractors. Do not prevent them from working with other clients, and do not try to control them. You want independence for yourself, so require independence for those that work with you.

Remember that you are hiring employees only because the project work you are taking on requires it, not because you are trying to create a team or a family. Your goals are wealth and independence, which means you are a solo businessperson who happens to engage with others to deliver on projects. You can help build their practice, and they can help you build your practice, but you are separate and independent. You are working together to help each other, and you want a long-lasting relationship with good people, but you don't want to create dependence or carry the weight of a resource that has no billable work.

Employee Paperwork

If you have employees, contract with a service provider that specializes in payroll. There are too many steps in creating paychecks on a monthly basis to make it worth your time to do it yourself, and it is very affordable to have someone do it for you (see Chapter 5 for more details about payroll). You'll spend a few hundred dollars a quarter for someone else to do it, versus many hours of your own time trying to do it yourself.

To make someone an official employee of your business, you need to complete the following paperwork. It should take only a few minutes to collect everything. Of course, you will want to consult with a CPA or payroll professional to ensure that you have everything required for your locality.

1. **Employment Eligibility Verification (USCIS Form I-9).** This has to be filled out by your employee to indicate whether they are a citizen or legally able to work in the United States. It takes only a few minutes to fill out.

2. **W-4.** This is the Employee's Withholding Allowance Certificate, and has to be filled out in order for the employer (you) to withhold federal tax. You will be paying the employee's federal and state taxes, and their paycheck from you will be post taxes. This can often come as a shock both to you, the employer (you'll have many direct transfers from your business checking account to the IRS), and to your employee (especially if they were formerly a subcontractor receiving pretax payments from you).

3. **Copies of identification.** Usually, a driver's license and a Social Security card are used, but there are other options.

Once you have these basic items on file, you have an official employee. You can start issuing payroll checks. You will have quite a bit of additional paperwork and forms that will be required (such as workers' compensation, quarterly reports, and insurance), which is why working with a payroll specialist and CPA is your best step. There is little reason why you would want to take ownership of this responsibility, as the costs are low to hire someone who specializes in it to handle it for you.

Your Responsibility to Your Employees

As previously stated, you have to make it abundantly clear to your employees that this is not a traditional employment role. You are working with them as independent parties who happen to have a formal employment relationship with you for contractual and tax purposes. You do not expect them to be subservient, and you do expect them to continue to operate with an independent, nonemployee mentality. You are working together to improve both of your businesses and to execute on project work that requires that you have certain paperwork and insurance in place. Your responsibility ends with this. You are not guaranteeing income, you are not working with them in a boss/employee relationship, and you are not providing benefits or other perks. In short, your responsibility is to ensure that both you and the person that you are employing understand this arrangement is virtually identical to a subcontractor role, except in the paperwork.

Conclusion

You have to plan for success, and expect it to happen. Planning for wealth in advance is important; guard yourself for a gathering storm. A storm can destroy you if you have a weak foundation, but its rains can cause growth and abundance if you are prepared and have built a strong foundation. The realities of growth in business usually require additional people to assist with your work. Rely heavily on a small team of subcontractors whose strengths and weakness you are familiar with, and who you can trust. If project work requires that you convert subcontractors to employees, move forward, but never take on a dependent and salaried employee. Be open with everyone, share as much detail as needed, and constantly keep your mind focused on your path to wealth and independence. As your business grows, always make sure you are doing nothing that will jeopardize your attainment of these two fundamental goals.

Business Investing and Wealth Utilization

The Abundance Mentality

The uncharitable do not go to the world of the gods; fools only do not praise liberality; a wise man rejoices in liberality, and through it becomes blessed in the other world.

—From *The Dhammapada*

There are two predominant mindsets about economics; one believes in riches and abundance, while the other sees only poverty and lack. The abundance mentality believes that there is more than enough of everything to go around for everyone, and that new wealth and material can be created. The poverty mentality believes that there isn't enough to go around, and that resources are finite and can only be consumed. As in all things, whichever mindset you lean toward manifests itself in the world around you.

If your worldview allows for infinite resources, your life will reflect this, and abundance will predominate. If your worldview sees limited resources, poverty will be your companion, regardless of the opportunities available to you. Your thinking is yours to control. You choose whether there is abundance or poverty in your life, and thereby influence how much abundance or poverty there is in your world.

There is such an abundance of opportunity, that everyone can have a piece, and no one has to go hungry. The fact that there are some who are hungry, who have less than what they need, is a sign that many are living with false views of the world, or have been hurt by or are under the influence of people with limited mentalities or wicked intentions. Certainly there is gross waste and negligence, consumption that far surpasses need, and signs that the world is bent on self-destruction. But if you look at the situation closely, you will see that these issues are localized, and often due to specific social environments. If the actions of the people in a particular environment were altered (especially when it relates to leadership), the resources would be restored and abundance would predominate.

Even if the opportunities were limited, you personally have the ability to create. From this creative potential comes new possibilities. If you believe in your ability to create something from where there was nothing, then you will always find more resources available and be able to generate greater things for others.

Your greatest tool in continuously growing your business and increasing your own personal wealth is to use your finances liberally. Someone who is generous, and who is constantly looking for ways to use the resources that come their way for the betterment of not only themselves but the everyone around them, is someone who will see constant opportunity and great levels of wealth, freedom, and success. The world needs people who live in abundance and generosity.

■ **Rule**　As long as there are people who are creating, there will be abundance. People who create jobs, new markets, and new ideas are critical to the health of economies and nations. In societies where ideas are suppressed and creative people are oppressed, the health of the nation suffers, and lack and hunger are the norm. In societies that support and enable the free exchange of ideas and the creative pursuits of individuals, material abundance flourishes.

Competition

You are not a competitor and you do not have competition. There may be others who are in the same business as you, and who could potentially take clients from you, but you should not view them as competition. Instead, view them as potential partners or collaborators. Anyone who is in the same business as you has the ability to help you grow, and you have the ability to help them grow. Any work you do together has the potential to create new opportunities, building something where nothing was before.

Figure 12-1 shows the traditional viewpoint that the pool of customers or opportunities from which to draw is finite. In this model, there is scarcity; any customer or work that you acquire is at the loss of either of your competitors, and anything they gain is your loss. This becomes an environment where your focus is on crushing your competitor so that you can continue to grow. It is a position of lack, and leads to negativity in thought and action. In this poverty-focused model, there is only one winner, the competitor who can acquire the most business. The customer, who is almost forgotten in the battle, is at the mercy of several parties who do not have the customer's best interests in mind, and are only at the table in order to scavenge what the others can't collect.

Figure 12-1. When competing, a finite pool of opportunities manifests

Figure 12-2 shows an entirely different model, one of infinite opportunity and partnership, where new work is created and new wealth is generated. It is a model where everyone wins: you, your partners, and the client. No one is trying to take anything from anyone else, and all are focused on creating a healthy and thriving environment in which the goal is the betterment of each other and the client. Instead of looking inward at a finite pool of opportunities and at each other with enmity, you and your partners are looking outward together, trying to create opportunities for each other and working with clients to expand scope and vision.

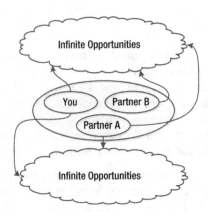

Figure 12-2. When partnering, infinite opportunities manifest

As an example of creating opportunities where none previously existed, consider a scenario where you are working with a client on a .NET application. You've been maintaining and expanding this application for several years, and the income is fixed at a certain number of hours or price per month. The client tells you that an integration initiative is starting, and they are looking for resources. You have integration skills, and know that you could potentially engage, but the client views you as a developer only.

You decide to reach out to one of your partners who specializes in integration, and have them interact directly with the client. You tell the partner that the opportunity is theirs to pursue, and that you expect no commission. You mention that if they need an extra hand in delivery, you are available, but otherwise you have no interest other than to see the client connected to a viable solution provider. In the end, the client hires the partner. Here is what is in it for you:

1. **You have created a new relationship**. You have created goodwill with both the client and the partner. They may create additional project work that may or may not include roles that you could take part in. Regardless of whether there is immediate work for you, you have elevated the relationship with both parties, and new conversations and opportunities can now arise.

2. **You are now a trusted advisor.** You have moved from being perceived as a "developer" by your client to being perceived as someone who has contacts, or even possibly as a trusted advisor (depending on how involved in the process you were). The client likely will turn to you in the future for recommendations and future project work.

3. **You have strengthened your partnership**. You have created an opportunity for your partner, so they now see you as someone they want to do more business with. If you bring people work, people will bring you work.

4. **You have been generous**. You have created an opportunity for someone else, without expectation of repayment. The energy that you've put into this will come back to you in unrelated ways. No kindness or act of generosity goes unnoticed by the powers that be.

View everyone as a potential partner, and as someone who either can help you or you can help. This is one of the best non-cash investments you can make in your business and in yourself. Be generous in all of your dealings, including sharing business and partnering in delivering better solutions to clients. This generosity will have an immeasurable impact on your success.

CASE STUDY

In the national market, I have a lot of partners using the same technologies and platforms that I use. I don't think of anyone as a competitor or a threat. I've had very good success working with other people to expand their businesses and mine at the same time, and virtually everyone I have worked with I view as a friend or a colleague.

The local market is limited, but there are some organizations that could benefit from some of the skills I have. Because the market is local, I often work at a very reduced rate, as I am interested in bringing high-end skills to a rural environment.

In the spirit of partnership, I reached out to a networking company that has a broad base of clients in the local market, asking the company if they would like to meet and discuss ways that we could potentially work together to bring a wider offering to their clients and to my clients. I saw it as a "win-win-win" situation, where all of us, including the clients, could benefit from additional expertise and knowledge.

The idea of competition was so strong in this company's mentality that they shut me down before I could even have a conversation. They perceived my reaching out as begging, and they thought I was going to try to steal their clients. Rather than having a conversation to see if I had something to offer that could benefit their business or their customers, they simply denied any conversation and essentially told me to take a hike.

My mentality is so antithetical to competition that this company's fear-based reaction was a surprise to me. What we believe is what we see in the world. If you view everyone as competition, you will always struggle for work, and will have evidence that others are taking your work. If you see everyone as a potential partner, you will always have an abundance of work and will be part of the creative process.

Investing in Your Business

Your business is your primary source of income. It is the engine that fuels your financial success, and supports your ability to pursue wealth and independence for use in nonbusiness activities. Always consider the health of your business to be of primary importance, and do not hold back on financially investing in it to make it stronger and more able to support you. If you expect to make $500,000 but are unwilling to invest $40,000 in a mentor to get you there, or $30,000 in a website and marketing material to make yourself look like a professional, or $15,000 in insurance to allow you to engage on a broader base of industries, then your expectations are outrageous and you will not be successful. You have to spend money to make money, and that spending starts with direct investments back into your business.

CASE STUDY

I received a quote for a major marketing initiative that I was interested in pursuing. The quote was for $40,000. I knew that if I engaged in this marketing, my business would grow, though I wasn't sure how. I signed the proposal and sent it over. Within two hours, I received an unsolicited inquiry for mentorship. In 24 hours, this was converted to a paid nine-month engagement that was worth $45,000 to me. Just by agreeing to spend $40,000 on my business, I was immediately reimbursed with a project of greater value that I was not expecting, and would most likely not have received had I not moved forward with the marketing project. The energy behind business is mysterious, yet ever present.

You have to approach situations in personal and professional life fearlessly and without limitations on your expectations. If you want substantial wealth and independence, you have to act like it is already yours. If you want to grow your income by 50% this year, then you have to be willing to spend 20% of your income to get you there. The investment is a one-time cost, while the growth to the next plateau is permanent (see the discussion of the sales plateau paradigm in Chapter 7).

Regardless of what amount of income you are making, a 20% investment is substantial. And, because it comes directly out of your pocket, it can be a difficult and nonintuitive step to take. When you are making $250,000 a year and you take $50,000 pretax dollars to execute on the goal of increasing your income in the future, it can feel like an extremely high-risk step to take. Yet, what you must realize is that much of business is risk taking, and when you are reaching for the height of what is possible to attain, you have to take many steps that others consider very risky.

Investing in Others

As your business grows, eventually you will need to hire subcontractors and possibly employees if a client requires you to do so. You will work with other businesses and partners on initiatives that can increase their revenue and your income. You will encounter people who you are interested in helping, either in a paid role or freely. As you work with others, always think of appropriate ways to invest in them, as the more you invest in others, the more success you will see.

Investing in Subcontractors and Employees

Here are several approaches to investing in people who work for or with you:

1. **Understand their goals**. Take an interest in each of the individuals who work with you, and try to understand their goals and ambitions. The more that you know about each person, the more you can help to direct things through you that will allow them to attain their goals. Also, the more focused and directed your employees and subcontractors are, the more success your business will see. If you know, for example, that a subcontractor's goal is to double their income, you can figure out ways that they can engage on multiple projects with you to increase their earnings.

2. **Align project work with interests**. You can work to sell projects that are in line with a subcontractor's interests. If you know what they want to work on, you can begin to mention it in business-level discussions with clients and prospects. Knowing that a subcontractor wants to engage in a certain type of technology is the first step in finding new work in that technology. If you aren't looking for something, you won't find it; knowing that a subcontractor is looking for work on a certain platform will often open doors to selling work on that platform.

3. **Give bonuses and perks**. You have a formula for paying your subcontractors. If things have gone well, give them a bonus. If they are on an extremely stressful project, send them on an all-expenses-paid weekend vacation. Invest in them to ensure that they are rewarded and remain energetic.

4. **Check in with everyone frequently**. When working with large firms, once you have started on a project, you rarely (if ever) get to talk with anyone from the staffing or consulting firm again. You are left to fend for yourself with the end client. Your subcontractors work with you, and you should plan to check in with them frequently to help out with code-related issues, gauge moral, and determine whether there is anything you need to do to address a situation.

Investing in Partners

Here are some ways to invest in the success of your partners:

1. **Think of their business first**. Improving a partner's business is one of the easiest ways to improve your own business. Partners often can sell larger projects than you can sell individually, and often at higher prices. They can also sell projects that require multiple resources, whereas you may be able to sell only one-or two-person projects as you are building your business. Your partners are often your primary channels to project work. You should have as much interest in the success and expansion of their business as you do in your own. Do everything you can to help support the growth of their business, and always think of what you can do to help them succeed and grow.

2. **Send business their way**. If you have a project offer that you cannot take, or that you could take but know that it would be implemented better by a larger firm or someone else who specializes in the technology, send that project opportunity to your partner. Think strategically about which of your partners would be the best fit and would provide the most value to your client. Try to take yourself out of the equation. If an opportunity opens for you on the project, that is a bonus, but it should not be a prerequisite to your sending business to your partner.

3. **Think of ways to improve relations**. Most of your partners will be large consulting or staffing firms. You may have a business relationship with one or more people within the company, but you likely won't have relationships with everyone. As you work on your own advertising and marketing to grow your own business, think of ways that you might be able to utilize this to

get to know other people within your partner's company. Perhaps historically you have done only integration work with your partner, but you know they also do SharePoint work. If you publish an article on SharePoint, or have a large potential project opportunity on the platform, try to initiate a conversation with the SharePoint lead at your partner's company.

4. **Offer to discuss strategies, marketing, etc**. You have your own advertising and marketing initiatives. In some cases, you may be able to utilize these to help your partner. Offer to write blog posts, talk with salespeople, meet with leads in their sales process (without cost), and anything else you can think of to help them create and sell work.

Investing in Clients

Your clients may be consulting or staffing firms where you work through them with their client, or they may be end clients that you do direct work with. Either way, the following are ways that you can invest in them to improve both your relationship and their ability to conduct business:

1. **Give a fair price**. You want your clients to prosper, and you want to engage with them for the long term. Figure out ways to make your pricing fair and reasonable. You need to make sure you are never considered an unnecessary expense. If you price yourself right, you are investing in your client and ensuring they have a long-term resource that will have their best interests in mind.

2. **Take an interest in their work or product**. Always be interested in the overall goals of the company and of the individual projects. There will certainly be tasks that you don't enjoy, and some troubleshooting and development work that will be a chore, but take a positive attitude and be thankful for the work. If you begin to dislike the work or to have a negative attitude toward the client's project, you are not providing value and need to figure out a way to extricate yourself from the situation.

3. **Take an interest in the people**. You will have the opportunity to develop professional relationships with many of the people you work with. Be sincerely interested in them, both in what they do professionally and what their personal plans and goals are. Sometimes employees of companies feel very marginalized, and you are a breath of fresh air from the outside. Bring your best to the table, and always engage with people. You can increase moral in the near term, and walk away with excellent contacts for the long term.

4. **Offer ideas for improvements**. Try to consult and not just develop. You've seen more in your project work across various clients than most employees will see in a lifetime. Bring your insight and skill to the table, and don't be afraid to share ideas for improvements. Some clients will be very closed to the idea of having you offer insights, and they will let you know right away that your place is as a developer and not as an advisor. Most clients, though, will welcome your insights.

5. **Deliver to the best of your ability**. Do everything with the best intention, and deliver the highest quality solutions you can give whatever circumstances you encounter. Some environments can be extremely challenging, but you must always work to deliver the best that you can.

6. **Part ways with the client when it is time**. There will come a time in most of your client relationships when it is time to part ways. The reason may be that the client no longer needs your skills, that the work is no longer appropriate for you, or any of a variety of other reasons. You will know when it is time to step away from a project, and though it may come as a small financial setback to you, and as a difficult transition for the client, it is a significant investment that will open new doors for you and the client. They will find someone who is fresh and excited about the work, and you will create a void in your schedule that will be filled by new work opportunities.

■ **Rule** You must learn to part ways with your least-desirable clients. Cutting clients is part of your path to success. You will have clients that you have outgrown, that are too demanding, that are unpleasant to work with, that don't respect you or your time, or that pay too little. As you end projects or relationships with clients, new opportunities will arise.

Investing in Personal Interests

How you spend your money on yourself (and your immediate family) has an influence on what happens to your business and what opportunities present themselves. Your lifestyle needs to reflect abundance, and reflect who you are. It does not need to be pretentious or ostentatious; you do not need to flaunt your money or spend it carelessly. It should reflect simplicity but be broad enough to allow you to create the kind of life that will allow you to flourish. If you are spending to show your wealth, or using your income frivolously, you may find that your success is short-lived and your fortunes are limited. If you are spending to grow into a bigger role that will allow you to achieve what you are on earth to do, then you will likely find that your success will grow and your finances will improve.

CASE STUDY

I was living in New Mexico with my wife and sons. After a series of incidents, my wife and I decided it was time to go back to our hometown and start a farm. We found some farmland close to town and put a contract on it. The cost was substantial, and was more than we were able to afford immediately. I knew, though, it was the right thing to do, and that if we purchased it, something would happen with my business that would enable us to afford it. We signed the contract, and within a month I landed a large, multi-resource project that was nowhere on the radar when we signed the contract. This is one of many examples I've experienced of creating work by creating a need. The platform (my business) is there to generate virtually any income necessary, but it requires that I expend energy and create a valid need. If I don't spend judiciously and with faith, projects do not come, and work begins to dry up. This spending must happen on many levels: within the business, within my personal life, and within charitable causes. If I sit on the money, things stagnate; I am forced to grow and give if I want my business to grow and continue to generate income.

Investing in Charity

With your eventual level of success and wealth, you will be in a position not only to donate money to existing charities, but also to set up your own charities. Make giving to causes that you do not directly benefit from one of the primary uses of your money. There is endless need in the world, and those who have received much have a responsibility to give much.

Much of your giving should be done in private. "So when you give to the needy, do not announce it with trumpets, as the hypocrites do in the synagogues and on the streets, to be honored by others. Truly I tell you, they have received their reward in full. But when you give to the needy, do not let your left hand know what your right hand is doing, so that your giving may be in secret" (Matthew 6:2). Some of your private (or anonymous) giving should be done through channels that are tax deductible, while other giving should be done with no expectations of returns. What you give should generally be no one's business but your own.

You should give with the understanding that the more you give, the more you will receive. The billionaires who have made the "Giving Pledge," which is a commitment to give most of their wealth to philanthropy, donate vast sums to charity, yet find that their net worth increases year over year. The more they give, the more their wealth seems to increase. This is the mystery of wealth; when spent on yourself, you never have enough to cover your debts, and you always require more. When spent on others, without expectation of anything back, you end up with more than you can give away.

■ **Rule** If you want to see the personal benefits of giving to charity, you need to give without expectation of remuneration. Try giving a sizeable chunk of money (for example, $20,000 if you are making $250,000 a year, $50,000 if you are making $500,000 a year) to a charity of your choice, and do it anonymously. By giving large sums, larger sums will come back to you. Make sacrifices and take risks if you want to see increased revenues that can support change in the world.

Approaches to Spending

While there are exceptions to every rule, generally speaking, as an individual in business by yourself, the energy and intent behind your use of money will impact how much wealth you can acquire. As Figure 12-3 shows, different types of spending cause either expansion or contraction of your net worth.

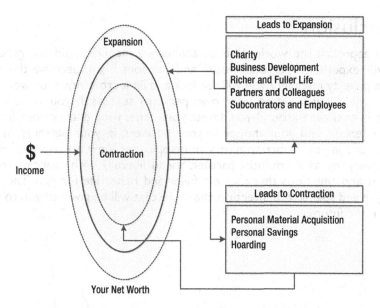

Figure 12-3. Spending contributes to either expansion or contraction of your net worth

Spending with an abundance mentality will increase your wealth, while spending with fear or with self-interest will decrease your wealth. Note the items in the following list as you determine how to spend your income:

1. If you take business money and invest it back in the business wisely, your business will grow and your profits will increase.

2. If you take business money and invest it in partners, colleagues, subcontractors, employees, and yourself (as a business party), they will experience growth and your relationships with them will strengthen.

3. If you take your profit and invest it in broadening your life and in charitable giving, you will increase your earning capacity and cause your wealth to increase.

4. If you hoard your business money, consider all of the profit yours, and can barely make ends meet off of the profit, you are living with a poverty mentality. You and your business will constantly struggle.

5. If you take your profit and spend it on yourself for more material wealth or put it in savings or retirement, you will limit your ability to grow, and will cause stagnation and shrinkage in your access to resources and to the growth of your business.

Conclusion

If you approach the world with an abundance mentality and are generous, you will experience personal wealth and freedom. If you perceive the world with a poverty mentality, you will see lack and limit creativity. Your worldview is incredibly important to your own personal success. If you want wealth, invest in everyone around you. Invest your time, your energy, your insights, your interests, and your money in your business, in your partners, in your clients, and in your subcontractors and employees. View no one as competition, everyone as a potential partner. Spend liberally with charities and on dreams and ambitions that create a fuller and richer life for you. The more you give and spend with intention, the more that will be given to you to work with in the future.

Health

Personal Vitality and the Impact on Your Business

The body is the servant of the mind. It obeys the operations of the mind, whether they be deliberately chosen or automatically expressed. At the bidding of unlawful thoughts the body sinks rapidly into disease and decay; at the command of glad and beautiful thoughts it becomes clothed with youthfulness and beauty.

—James Allen, *As a Man Thinketh*

If you want to be an employee of an organization, your mental and physical health are largely irrelevant to the success or failure of the business you work for. If, however, you are working to run the most efficient and productive independent practice that you can, then your mental and physical health are of the utmost importance. You are aiming for wealth and independence, both of which can be achieved only if you are operating at your highest potential. You can operate at your highest potential only if you are healthy in mind and body. This chapter outlines a number of approaches to keeping yourself mentally and physically fit. You'll find that it is a process of experimentation and constant dedication.

■ **Rule** Decision making and discernment of right action require peak mental health and basic levels physical fitness. You will not be able to make the best choices in business or in personal matters unless you are committed to being healthy in mind and body.

You have to take your health seriously for a number of reasons, but two directly relate to your business. First, to run your own business and achieve high levels of wealth and independence through your work, you have to operate continuously at your highest capacity, both mentally and physically. You will be required to deliver in a highly efficient manner, with client deliverables, advertising material, sales calls, and meetings. You have to be in excellent shape to work your way through your day successfully.

Second, your mental and physical state will directly impact your business; if you are disorganized and in poor health, your business will reflect the same. If you have strength and vitality, your business will have a foundation from which it can thrive. You cannot separate the health of your person from the success of your profession. You are your business, and your health is the health of your business.

When you meet with clients, they expect to be working with the best available resource. If you appear to be in poor physical condition, clients may conclude that you don't have time to take care of yourself, much less build the best solution for them. You have to be able to take care of yourself before you can take care of others. Potential clients will determine what kind of code and solution you can build for them based on your appearance, your mannerisms, and your conversation.

CASE STUDY

When you go to get your haircut, you can assess how your hair is going to look afterward by observing the stylist's hair. If the stylist has a bad haircut, then you can pretty much guarantee that you will get a bad haircut.

I once went to a dentist to have a routine checkup. The dentist reeked of cigarette smoke. I never went back. How can I trust someone who smokes to tell me how to take care of my oral health?

I've known a number of preachers who are extremely worldly in nature...fast cars, copious alcohol, and numerous former husbands or wives. What guidance can this person provide?

There are professionals in all walks of life that are not living healthy or productive personal lives, and it greatly impacts their ability to be successful in their chosen professions. If they can't take care of themselves, how can they take care of others?

In your career, you want to make strong and positive impressions that propel you past initial judgments into immediate progress on business. If you want to improve the speed of your sales cycle, cut through any reservations that a client has about working with you, and ensure that you are delivering at your highest potential, then you need to cultivate your physical health and presence. Eating well and keeping fit are sure ways to build a foundation that can handle the type of success you are working to achieve, and instill confidence in those around you that you are disciplined and thoughtful enough to help them achieve the results they are looking for.

Being healthy physically and mentally does not require a vigorous dedication to working out, but it does require taking time to exercise on a regular basis, eat well, and be conscious of your activities and how they impact your physical and mental health. It also requires knowing how to balance your work with your goals, deal with stress, and step away from the office without taking a huge financial hit. The path to true wealth and independence requires work, sacrifices, and constant dedication to being healthy and keeping yourself that way.

Dealing with Stress

Your project work will lead to regular cycles where you should expect to encounter standard stresses. Working on multiple projects simultaneously requires organization, focus, and energy. Being in business for yourself in a fast-paced environment is naturally stressful. There will be times when timelines, deliverables, support requirements, or deployments will cause your stress to increase for a period of time, and will be present until you have completed the outstanding tasks.

You may also have times where your sales activity has diminished, and your future work pipeline is weak. Having too much work or too little work are both very common for the independent coder, and both lead to their own kind of stress. These periods of stress may last for days or weeks. The following list outlines a number of approaches for managing stress throughout these cycles:

1. **Take time to sleep.** This is very basic advice, but many people don't take it seriously. If you expect to perform at your best, you have to get enough sleep. The investment in sleep pays off in performance. Consider your work to be similar to an intense physical workout. You have to be alert, focus on multiple projects at once, deliver in a rapid and efficient manner, and constantly be ready for prompt communications. There will be times when you cannot get as much sleep as you need because of various obligations, but if you are chronically lacking enough sleep, you will never achieve your best output and you and your business will suffer. Lack of sleep will cause standard situations to become stressful, and stressful situations to become completely unmanageable.

2. **Utilize your time efficiently.** When you are at work, spend time only on business-related activities. There is no time in your workday to spend on anything other than building your business or delivering on work. If you have a few minutes where there simply is nothing to work on, walk away from your office and get some fresh air. If you do not manage your time efficiently, you will never have enough time to get things done, and you will always remain under stress. Fight to stay on top of your work, restrain from overdelivering, and make sure you aren't engaged in busywork.

3. **Make a list.** Make a list of things that you need to get done. Write things down, just as you would when you are goal setting (see Chapter 10). After you have written down your to-do list, you no longer have to think about what is left to do, as you can refer to it on paper. Having things out of your head and captured on paper is one of the easiest ways to free up your mind to focus on more important issues, like getting things done. If you never write down your tasks, you will constantly be under stress trying to remember what it is you need to do.

4. **Prioritize your free time.** There must be an end to your workday. When that time comes, close up shop. Keep your phone with you to stay on top of e-mails and high-priority phone calls, but leave your delivery work behind. You should always be available in case an urgent matter arises or you receive a sales call, but your free time is as important as your work time. If you never leave your office, or leave it only if work permits, you will burn yourself out.

5. **Make forward progress with tasks.** It is easy to get overwhelmed when a large amount of work has piled up. Make sure that regardless of the demands, you are constantly making forward progress. You must be diligently completing tasks and deliverables and pursuing new sales and project opportunities even as deadlines near and client demands for your time increase. Making even small gains on the work that needs to be done will slowly get you through the difficult times.

6. **Take frequent breaks.** Regardless of the calls you have scheduled or the demands placed on you by clients and others, you have to step away from your desk and walk around. Sitting without movement for hours at a time will cause stagnation in your mind and body, and the stresses of the moment will have no way to dissipate. Force yourself to step away from your computer every hour or so, take a quick walk, and reassess whether what you are working on is getting you closer to completing a task and reducing the number of tasks overall and, in turn, your level of stress.

7. **Turn off your technology.** During periods of high demand and high stress, it is even more important to block out time where you are not working. Your business is based on your responsiveness and availability, but at the same time you must be able to turn off your technology (and therefore access to you) long enough to recover. The easiest thing to do is to set aside the weekend and turn off your phone. A lengthy period of time without having to read e-mail or think about work is in order during periods of high stress. You do not need to do this all of the time, but it is critical during highly stressful times to schedule downtime.

8. **Eat well and exercise.** Times of stress require that you make an extra effort to care for yourself physically. Eat better than you usually would. Take time to prepare a fresh meal at home. Drink water to cleanse your system. Take a walk, go for a jog, get out into nature. Sections later in this chapter provide more specific ideas related to diet and exercise.

9. **Communicate with others.** If your client situation is stressful on a continual basis, you need to discuss the issue with your client. Communicate with your team members to see if anything can be changed to help you better manage the stress. If you are on a good project, people will be happy to strategize with you about how to change your role or lighten the stress. If you are on a bad project, you'll come to realize that no one cares about your health or well-being, and you need to figure out how to extricate yourself.

Rule You can set limits on how you are utilized. Many projects require that people on the team work around the clock during periods of troubleshooting, testing, or deployment. You can expect to work long hours a day here or there, but if you find yourself on a project that forces you into an unhealthy pattern of work, it's time to make a change. When people are forced to work late into the night, their morale declines and their inefficiencies increase. Do not allow yourself to be used in this manner. Set expectations and limits to your involvement. Set a certain time or a certain number of hours after which you turn off the computer, inform your team you will see them in the morning, and leave. Your skills are what show your value and help the team, not the number of hours you work.

10. **Eliminate the cause of the stress.** Sometimes, you will have a client or a project that is continually stressful. Many corporate cultures push their people to work long hours, and others have unrealistic expectations and poor management. If a client causes you constant stress, you have to cease doing business with them. You need to do so responsibly, especially if you are subcontracting through another company. Give adequate notice and help smooth the transition so that you don't leave anyone in a difficult place, but figure out an exit strategy and act on it quickly.

CASE STUDY

Much of my work is subcontracted through larger partner firms. When working directly with clients, I have a lot of control, and rarely end up in a stressful situation that can't easily be changed. However, when subcontracting, especially through large consulting firms, I have less control over projects and am often part of a team. These projects often require heavy levels of commitment, and the end client often expects contract workers to work late nights and weekends when the client deems that the project timeline requires it. In these cases, I set expectations early in the process that I will have to limit the majority of my work to business hours, and that only in certain circumstances will I be able to work late nights. If the client refuses to accept these requirements, I remove myself from the project.

Vacations

When you are employed by someone, the employer typically guarantees vacation time, and almost always paid. When you work for yourself, however, taking a vacation can be extremely difficult and costly. The cost can be exorbitant. If you are making $1,500 a day, and you decide to turn off your computer and disappear for a week, you lose $7,500 in billable revenue. Additionally, taking time off can impact your retainer relationships and put a strain on sales, deadlines, and work in general. If you can stay in contact with clients, remain visible, and keep basic momentum going with development and sales work, these costs and stresses can be minimized (or in some cases, eliminated). The billable vacation is often the independent coder's best option.

Rule Stepping out of the office for a day often means you have two days of catch-up work to do. Stepping out for a week can mean setting yourself up for a highly stressful return to work, where catching up may require extensive overtime. Your goal when planning a vacation is to maximize your time off and minimize your labor when you return. Staying in contact and doing a minimal amount of work each day ensures that you remain billable and reduce the amount of catch-up you have to do once you are back in the office.

Following are the nine steps to planning and taking a billable vacation:

1. **Ensure that you can do all of your client work remotely.** Flexibility to plan working vacations is another excellent reason not obligate yourself to business travel on a regular basis. If you can do your work remotely, it doesn't matter whether you are in your office or in a temporary vacation rental on the beach.

2. **Make sure you are 100% mobile.** All of your development machines should be high-end laptops. You should be able to pack up and go to any location that has internet connectivity at any time.

3. **Work early mornings.** If you have family with you, you can get most of your work out of the way before everyone else is ready to get up and go. Working three or four hours in the early morning will enable you to stay on top of e-mails, take care of basic monitoring and support, and likely complete some development.

4. **Be selective in which clients know you are on vacation.** You should have a mix of project work that includes retainers, fixed hourly, high stress, and low stress. Many of your clients do not need to know that you are going to be on a partial vacation, as it will not impact your ability to support them or deliver at the same level you have been delivering. Other clients (especially the time intensive or hourly) need to know that you will have limited availability, but that you will be continuing to work on their projects to ensure that there is forward momentum. Your goal with your billable vacation is to continue to bill clients, but not at the same level you do during regular working weeks. You need to slow down temporarily, but keep the income and momentum flowing. Scale back only on the work that is too time intensive to allow for this.

5. **Respond instantly.** Your business is based largely on your being available. Sales and new project opportunities come and go rapidly. Keep your phone with you during your vacation, and always respond promptly to e-mails and phone calls. If the communication requires that you complete some work, simply give them a timeframe for delivering it, and go back to your time off. If the communication is about new work, let them know you are available at any time to discuss it. You can remain engaged with a minimum of effort, as long as you manage your time and let people know that you won't be able to get to major pieces of work until later.

6. **Set expectations.** You may need to let some of your "needier" clients know that you will be traveling and may be offline portions of the day. You can set meeting times with them in advance, if necessary. As long as you let them know you will have gaps in availability, they should understand. You may need to inform extremely needy clients that you will be entirely unavailable during your time off.

7. **Be ambiguous.** No one needs to know where you are, where you are working from, or why you are away. If appropriate, let clients know that you are traveling, but you don't need to offer more information. You will be interacting with clients daily and continuing to work, so you don't need to call it a "vacation" (because it is not a true vacation). There is no value for the client to know that you are working from an office next to the beach rather than from your regular office. Don't share more information than is necessary.

8. **Expense the trip.** If you are taking a working vacation, you can expense most of the costs to your business. Additionally, if you have a client meeting in the vicinity of your destination, you may be able to share some of the costs with the client. Many clients are used to paying round-trip airfare and lodging, and may be open to covering expenses, as long as you can create a viable reason for needing to meet with them onsite.

9. **Find a new client.** Wherever you are, there are opportunities. Anytime you travel, be on the lookout for new clients and new ways to engage with people. If you put the energy and thought out there, you will very likely uncover some work. Always check your network before any vacation to see if you have any contacts in the area who it may make sense to reach out to.

CASE STUDY

Frequently, when I am traveling on vacation, I am able to expand my network of business contacts and active clients. A number of years ago, I was traveling in Argentina. I had taken a couple of weeks off of work, and was deep in the country. I started a conversation with an individual, and soon he was asking if I could do some work for him. The work led to a small U.S.-based engagement that covered the costs of the trip in its entirety.

On a separate occasion, several years ago, I took my wife and two boys (one an infant, the other a three-year-old) to the beach for five weeks. We rented a vacation house, and I set up office in a temporary space. When the boys were sleeping or napping, I worked, and was able to put in five- or six-hour days without issue (early mornings and midafternoons). During the five weeks that I was there, I met with several clients I had in the region, and ended up with a new project that started while I was there, and lasted for several months. The project work brought in revenue that I would not have found had we not been in the area for an extended period. Because I was working throughout, I was able to expense the whole trip. My revenue was constant, the costs of the trip were minimized, a new client opportunity was uncovered, and I was able to spend more than a month away from home with my family walking on beaches for the better part of the day.

Diet

Mohandas Gandhi, in his autobiography *The Story of My Experiments with Truth*, wrote about a number of different approaches he took to fasting and diet. He spent much of his life experimenting with how different diets influenced his mental state and impacted his interior and exterior life. In his later years, he ate no more than five unique types of food a day, and severely restricted his caloric intake. You don't have to take things to this extreme, but you do need to understand the importance of experimenting with your diet. Experiment until you find a diet that sustains you in a healthy way and provides the energy you need to support your focus on strong delivery and business growth.

Rule Don't underestimate the effect that food has on your ability to perform at your highest level. If you fuel your body with garbage, your output will be similar. Support high-quality output with high-quality food. There is more truth to the adage "you are what you eat" than you may think.[1]

Everyone knows the basics of proper nutrition, yet the majority of people have terrible diets. So, too, the majority of people are not operating at their highest capacity. You are running a race that you want to win; the prize is wealth and independence, and mastery of your professional trade. If you want to win, you have to take steps to tune yourself and perfect your performance.

There are millions of cars on the streets and in garages in varying conditions. Most of these cars can be used for basic transportation and daily travel, but only the finest among them could compete successfully in a race. Those that could win the race have been tuned and built to win. You have to ensure you are giving yourself the foundation of fitness you need to win the race that you are in.

There are endless ideas about what constitutes a proper diet. The key for you is to experiment to determine what is best for *you*. Different projects and stages in life will require different approaches to diet. Although many different diets will work (and you likely have your own preferences and opinions), you must experiment until you find a diet that gives you the energy to achieve the level of success, wealth, freedom, and independence you seek.

---

[1]See *Gastroenterology* 2013 Jun; 144(7): 1394–1401 for more information on how the health of your gut has a direct impact on your mental health.

Sugar

Many coders are dependent on soda pop and candy. One of the worst things you can do to yourself is to regularly consume sugary beverages and snacks. How many developers do you know who have stacks of Mountain Dew in a refrigerator next to their computers? The combination of sugar and caffeine can fatigue you in the short term and lead to serious issues in the long term. Clarity of thought is critical in your pursuit of your goals and dreams, and thought can't be clear if drowned in a sugary syrup on a constant basis.

Vegetables and Meat

Try a diet consisting almost entirely of vegetables. Some meat in your diet can certainly invigorate you, but excluding it from most of your meals will cleanse you. The cleaner your body is, the cleaner and more lightweight you will find your thinking to be. Find a good online recipe provider for specific types of meals, and subscribe to their service. Try a radical vegetarian or vegan diet for a short period of time (30 days) to see whether it increases your work output. Eat a steak once every week or two, but otherwise go green.

Caffeine

A large number of coders survive off of caffeine. Coffee is a staple diet. Red Bull and other energy drinks are a necessity. Weaning yourself off of caffeine may seem impossible, but you will be surprised how well a clean system works once caffeine is no longer part of it. You'll be alert the moment you wake up, and you'll produce substantially more without it then you did when you were dependent on it. Try liberating yourself from caffeine to see what you are capable of without its influence.

Snacks

Snacking throughout the day is a sure way to reduce your productivity and impact your health negatively. When you go into a workplace with a large IT department, invariably you will find piles of candy, chips, pop, and every other kind of junk food. People who consume snacks throughout the day are trapping themselves. You cannot reach your highest potential if you are consuming, on a constant and ongoing basis, large quantities of pure garbage. Throw out the snacks, and limit yourself to two or three meals per day. Eat at meal time, and give your system a chance to recover between meals. Note that the elimination of snacking includes all types of food, even celery.

Drugs and Alcohol

Legal and illegal, alcohol and drugs are the bane of the independent mind. If your primary goals are wealth and independence, success for your business, attainment of your personal dreams and ambitions, and living at your maximum potential, you will achieve these goals most easily if you are sober and clean. Eliminating foreign substances from your mind and your body will have a significant effect on your physical, mental, and spiritual state of being. Very few people strive for the sober life, and very few people achieve their dreams. Not everything that society embraces is useful or beneficial, especially when you are trying to break away from the pack and engage in life on your own terms.

■ **Rule** Independence is a separation from others, and a reliance on yourself. Your pursuit of independence should include not only your freedom from the rules and dictates of people in your professional and personal life, but also freedom from substances. Dependence on food or drugs is a massive hindrance for those who are pursuing true independence and freedom in their lives.

Exercise

If you want movement and growth in your business, you have to have movement and growth in your body. Your body is a conduit between the physical world and your mind. If the conduit is unhealthy, static, and out of shape, the path between your mind and the external world will be blocked, and your ability to see your thoughts and ideas materialize will be limited. In addition to enabling you to better support the manifestation of your ideas through your business, being in a fit physical state enables you to manage your stress better and focus more sharply on what you need to accomplish.

Often, developers fall into one of two camps. The first camp includes the sedentary, highly out-of-shape developer who survives on coffee and soft drinks, rarely emerging from the basement. The second includes the extreme athlete who participates in ultra-marathons and has a strict approach to diet, coding only long enough to cover the costs of their next adventure.

If you fall into either of these camps, you likely won't be able to achieve the fullest potential of wealth and independence available to you. Individuals in the first camp have no concern for their own well-being, and likely don't have the stamina or inclination to achieve great things through their business or in their lives. Individuals in the second camp have higher priorities than their business; their sport comes first, and everything else a distant second.

Their discipline and health would allow them to achieve great results in whatever they do, but their interests lie outside of their business. As Figure 13-1 illustrates, too little or too much focus on physical fitness can be counterproductive to the success of your business.

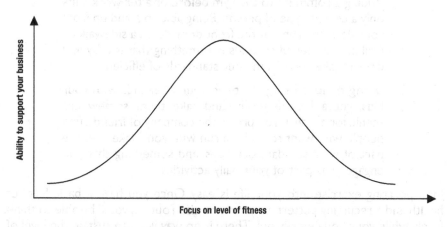

Figure 13-1. Too little or too much focus on fitness will impact your business negatively

You want to find the proper balance between your focus on exercise and your focus on your business (and the rest of your life). The following list outlines several ways to find this balance:

1. **Make it constant**. Make exercise part of your daily routine. You need to stay active throughout the day, and work movement into your life. Signing up for the gym and going for only two weeks won't do anything for you. Ongoing, constant dedication to basic levels of movement and fitness is the steady requirement to the ongoing, constant building of your business and freedom.

2. **Set a time**. Dedicate a certain time period to your exercise. Make it part of your daily routine, and respect it like you would a meeting with a client. You have to make your exercise time a priority, or you will always find something else to attend to.

3. **Determine what works for you**. Some people like team sports, others like independent pursuits. Based on your interests, figure out what type or types of exercise you can stick to for the long term. You need to be able to participate year round, regardless of the season, so you may want to choose different types of exercise for different seasons.

4. **Keep it simple.** You need to engage in something that is easy for you to pursue. For instance, you can walk or run in virtually any setting. Choose an activity that doesn't require a lot of gear, and that you can do in a moment. Adding a commute to the gym before or after work suits only a certain type of person. Being able to stand up from your desk and run out the front door down a sidewalk or trail in a matter of seconds is something that is easy and doesn't take away from your standards of efficiency.

5. **Bring others in.** If you spend your weekends with your kids, get a bicycle trailer and take them somewhere scenic for a ride. If you prefer the company of friends, find people who want to go for a run with you. Make exercise part of your standard activities, and something that you engage in as part of your daily activities.

Incorporating exercise into your life is easy. Once you have a basic level of health and a recurring pattern to your exercise routine, you'll be able to think freely while your body works out. There is no way you can sustain the level of concentration and efficiency that will be required of you for your pursuit of wealth and independence unless you are physically fit and healthy.

CASE STUDY

I generally start my workday at 4:30 AM. I work for an hour or two and then go for a 20- or 30-minute run. I always run before the dawn breaks. In the darkness, I run down the road, and along desert trails. The stars or moon illuminate the path just enough to see. The only sounds are owls and coyotes. During my runs I plan my day, think through problems that I am trying to solve, and decompress. Once the run is over, I spend some more time working before I head out for breakfast. By the time 8 AM rolls around and clients start to call and e-mail, I've already worked for two or three solid hours, have gotten my exercise in, and have eaten breakfast with my kids and wife.

Conclusion

Performing at your highest capacity requires a healthy lifestyle. This chapter outlined basic approaches to dealing with stress, taking a vacation, experimenting with diet, and engaging in exercise. There is no single approach to any of these that will work perfectly at all times for everyone. Health is not about a specific routine, but instead is about constant, ongoing experimentation and tuning in response to various stimuli in your personal and professional life. You have to decide how important the goals of wealth and independence are to you, and you also need to set parameters around what it means to achieve these. Your business is successful if it supports your ambitions and your dreams, and if you are free to pursue what you are truly passionate about. Your business is not successful if you are tied to it, it jeopardizes your health, or you are not achieving goals and dreams that you have set for yourself.

Freedom Through Business

Wealth, Dreams, and Independence

Happiness is not fame or riches or heroic virtues, but a state that will inspire posterity to think in reflecting upon our life, that it was the life they would wish to live.

—Herodotus, *The Histories*

You are engaged in a profession that is unlike any other. You can work from anywhere, make a sizeable amount of money, and alter the course of your business and work to support your personal interests, goals, and dreams. Having this level of freedom with business is extremely rare. You have the opportunity to take your life in virtually any direction you choose. You have the responsibility to use your wealth wisely, dream big, and utilize your independence to do great things.

Rule You cannot have more freedom in any professional trade than you can today as an independent coder in business for yourself. Assuming you put into practice the various procedures outlined in this book, you can live anywhere you want, and can move at a moment's notice. You can pursue what interests you, and increase your income overnight if you need to have more purchasing power. You can change your life and the lives of people around you through action and altruism. Don't trivialize this freedom; most people will never have a chance to experience anything like it.

To be successful as an entrepreneur, you must have a deep desire to accomplish your goals and a deep commitment to your business. Your business has to be your primary focus. This doesn't mean that you have to sacrifice your life for your business, but it does mean that you have to set aside the time and the energy to ensure that you are doing what is necessary for it to grow and support you. Realize that your business, as an independent coder, is your engine to generate the type of financial prosperity you need in order to reach your goals. Your business is an extension of you, so making it a primary focus is equal to making yourself your primary focus.

If you have only marginal interest in your trade, or you don't have the energy to devote to building your business, then you can't achieve true wealth or independence through it. In order to succeed, you must:

1. Have sincere dedication and focus.

2. Take all aspects of your business seriously.

3. Be disciplined.

4. Invest in your ongoing education with time and money.

5. Be ethical.

6. Have an intelligent approach to advertising, selling, networking, and setting fees.

7. Know how to put together contracts, grow your business, and work with others.

8. Have a plan in place for how you will use your wealth.

9. Know how to execute on your goals.

10. Keep yourself healthy.

If you are lacking any of these, you reduce your ability to rise above the crowd and enter into a class of your own.

Defining Wealth and Success

Throughout this book the concepts of wealth and success have been discussed extensively. The two are largely interchangeable. You are wealthy if you have abundance, and you are successful if you have abundance. Having a great deal of money does not necessarily mean you have abundance; therefore, money does not constitute wealth or success, though it is generally a factor in both.

Wealth and success are a combination of professional and personal matters; a wealthy businessperson may have a chaotic family life, and a successful parent may struggle to make ends meet. Each has arrived at success within a portion of their lives, but neither is both wealthy and successful in all aspects. Your goal, which is entirely attainable, should be to achieve wealth and success in all aspects of your life. Once you have attained this, your ability to create a better world for you and those around you will be limitless.

To be truly wealthy and successful, you have to meet a number of criteria. In the end, though, meeting this criteria is a matter of personal definition. You must gauge how far you have come from you started, determine whether you have achieved your goals and dreams, and evaluate how you are living your life to determine whether you are wealthy and successful. The following are several ways to measure your wealth and your success:

1. **Quality of life.** Are you living life as you want to? Do you have ample time to spend with your children, your spouse, your friends, yourself? So many people are dissatisfied with their circumstances. They don't like their job, they have difficult commutes, they are never home; they are a victim of the environment around them, and feel powerless to change. In your case, you should have no complaints about the quality of your life. If you are successful, you have full control over your situation, and can determine how you live. If you have any complaints, and you cannot do something about them, then you are not truly successful.

2. **Ability to pursue personal interests.** With wealth comes the ability to pursue your interests. If you dream of retirement so that you have time to do the things you've always wanted to do, you are not presently wealthy. Being able to execute and engage in things that you are passionate about today is a sign that you have reached true wealth. A successful person can pursue their passions and interests while maintaining their income and their business.

3. **Abundance of time**. Many people despise the corporate life because of how it consumes time. Do you manage your time well? Are you the master of your time and how it is used? If you have an abundance of time, and can take part in the activities you choose to, then you have attained a level of success few achieve.

4. **Mentally stimulated.** Your work should be challenging and mentally rewarding. Any of your individual projects, standing on their own, may be of limited interest to you, but as a whole, your business should always be stimulating. There are many people in the corporate world who are not mentally stimulated at all. They trudge to their cubicles and monotonously go through their daily work. At the end of the workday, they commute home, exhausted, and collapse, only to do it again the next day. They are not learning, they are not growing. They are wasting away while life passes them by. You, on the other hand, will have the chance to engage at every moment of the day. If you are not mentally stimulated, you are neither wealthy nor successful.

5. **Constant growth and change**. The projects you engaged on three years ago should look very different from the projects you engage on today. The conversations you have with clients and in your personal life should reflect ever-increasing wisdom and insight. Your life should be expanding, your opportunities growing, and your ability to help others increasing all of the time. If you are not changing for the better, then you are moving away from success rather than into it.

6. **Financially rewarded**. Of course, money is an aspect of wealth and success. You will be working alone, often remotely, and receiving a check may be your only sign that you are doing work that people value. If a client continues to send a check, then you can assume they are pleased with your work. You have skills that the world is looking for, and you have the ability to help others build their businesses and their infrastructures. You deserve to be paid, and to have the freedom to work with as many clients as you can so that you can keep your rates reasonable and your profit high. If you aren't making money as a technologist, and you aren't thinking of ways you can increase your output to increase your income, then you are not pursuing wealth or success; you are not even trying.

7. **Nonmaterialistic.** If you are materialistic, can only be happy with the acquisition of things, and try to distinguish yourself through consumer-based products, you are neither wealthy nor successful. If you lost all of your material possessions today, how would you react? Some people end their lives after financial ruin. If you consider material loss a setback, but otherwise would be unchanged by it and could be happy with your lot whether you have financial prosperity or not, you can consider yourself successful. Enjoy your money, and use it to enrich your life and your world, but don't get tied to it. Recognize it for what it is, and keep your happiness separate from it. "No one can serve two masters. Either you will hate the one and love the other, or you will be devoted to the one and despise the other. You cannot serve both God and money," wrote the Apostle Matthew. Money and material possessions are not inherently evil, but they can certainly draw you away from what is truly important.

8. **Able to give back.** Are you setting aside money to give to charity, both public and private? Do you have interests that are outside of yourself, and that build others without direct reimbursement to you? Your willingness to give to others is a sign of your character. You don't have to be wealthy to give, but if you are wealthy and successful, then you are able to give in ways that others could not. If you give freely and generously, you can consider yourself wealthy and successful.

Your Responsibility to Dream

With wealth and success, you have the ability to achieve virtually anything you want. You will not have to struggle with finances, and you won't have to dedicate yourself to a job that you dislike, or that does not reflect your personal values. With this level of freedom, you have the responsibility to have dreams that are big, and that are greater than simple materialistic gain.

True dreams appear impossible to attain, and have no clear path to completion (unlike goals). They are ephemeral and difficult to describe. They often challenge the perceived realities of the world, and are generally something we keep to ourselves. A person with a dream is alive; the spark of life is in them, and they have the chance to do something great in this world. A person without a dream is in the process of dying, and has lost their ability to achieve something great.

Often, dreams are forgotten in youth, and it is not uncommon for adults to have only dim notions of what their purpose is. Goals can be challenging to define, and dreams even more so. Dreams are the thought manifestation of what your true purpose is. If you have a dream, pursue it with everything you have. If you do not have a dream, pursue discovering one with everything you have. Define what you would do if you could do anything in your life, and then set out to do that thing. The following list outlines several key factors in being able to successfully define and pursue your dreams:

1. **Seek solitude.** You must spend time alone to find out who you truly are and what you seek in life. Substantial amounts of solitary time are required for thought and reflection. If you are not spending consistent time alone, away from distractions, you will never discover what you really want to achieve in your life. Set aside time to be alone in an environment that is conducive to silence and thought. Seek clarity and purpose to identify what you are after. Seek guidance and insight in order to pursue what you are after.

CASE STUDY

When I am in need of major changes within my life, either private or professional, I head into nature and focus on the change required. An excellent example of a trip that provided significant results occurred last summer. One evening I drove my motorcycle deep into the desert hills near the town that I live in. I rode until the dirt road ended. I parked my bike, and hiked into the juniper trees. I laid out my sleeping bag under the stars on the side of an adobe hill. I spent time deep in thought, listening. When I returned home in the morning, I had answers to my questions, and in the coming weeks I achieved positive results from pursuing the changes that I contemplated during this time in solitude. When it comes to defining who you are and determining what your goals and dreams are, there is nothing more powerful than being alone in nature, far from technology, with no one and nothing around.

2. **Engage in the present.** Many people have dreams but are unwilling to take steps in the present that could help them manifest. Often, people will not work a job that they consider beneath them or their ideals, and choose to be idle rather than engaged. However, by working in any capacity in the present, you will discover opportunities that enable you to pursue your dreams. Your dreams may be lofty, and require that you have resources to achieve them. Your goals of wealth and independence are stepping stones for you to be able to achieve your dreams.

3. **Solidify your foundation.** Your philosophy and understanding of life need to be deep, and you need to continue to build on them until you have a firm foundation that will support you through all challenges, personal and professional. Trying to identify and pursue your dreams without a solid framework will be fruitless. You must have a firm sense of self and know your place in the world in order to successfully define your dreams.

4. **Push yourself.** "If your dreams don't scare you, they aren't big enough," said Ellen Johnson Sirleaf. You have one chance at life. Are you working to leave a legacy, or simply to recreate and relax? You must set high expectations for yourself, and go after end results that will challenge you and force you to grow and change. If your dreams are not lofty enough, you won't achieve what you are capable of.

5. **Talk with people.** Engage with people outside of your circle. So many people are stuck within a certain social structure, where there is neither interest nor opportunity to talk with people who come from different backgrounds or have different views and experiences. Much of our learning comes from people, and if we are interacting only with those who are familiar to us, then we have a limited pool of ideas. You want to seek interactions with many types of people, both to gain insight into how different characters and personalities function, and to try to apply what you learn from them to defining your own goals and ambitions. Seek out people who you haven't engaged with before. Their ideas and conversations will spark new thoughts in you. Dreams are thoughts.

6. **Explore.** When traveling in any foreign country, inevitably you will find that you have been herded onto a "tourist path." Somehow, without planning it, you'll end up in the flow of people who are touring, and you'll see only what they see. Once you have entered the tourist path, you will see a lot of popular attractions and make new acquaintances, but you will no longer be exploring or finding anything that others haven't seen many times before you. Life is like this; you have to work hard to escape the tourist path that everyone is following. You have to break from friendships and from patterns to find something new and to pursue great things. Exploring and seeking what is difficult to find and hidden from view is essential in your ability to define and pursue your dreams.

7. **Learn**. A lifelong commitment to learning is essential. Most dreams are conceived in youth. If you are not continuously learning and trying to apply what you have learned to the pursuit of your dreams, they will die or go dormant. Dreams will mature as you mature and as you nurture and support them. Reading, researching, discussing, writing, and seeking are all part of the process in manifesting your dreams.

8. **Experiment**. Assume that everything you have been taught is a lie, and that all of the information you and others believe is true isn't. Validate and test every idea and every theory that is not your own. Experiment with different approaches, different ways of living, and different ideas. Don't believe experts, don't trust in science, don't accept others' interpretations of religion, politics, history, or your origins and purpose. Investigate and search; by doing this, you will uncover truths that you never could have found otherwise, and you will come to an understanding of the world that is your own. With this, your dreams will come to you naturally.

True Independence

The world needs independent thinkers, and people who go against the tide of society. If you are doing what everyone else is doing, you are not independent, even if you are working for yourself. People (in business and in private life) need someone to tell them the truth, to have a unique perspective, and to not be afraid to say what needs to be done. You will be of infinitely more value to your clients, yourself, and the world if you are able to see things for what they are and communicate your understanding and perceptions. You can consider yourself truly independent if you have the following characteristics:

1. **Come to your own conclusions**. Forget what is proper and convenient, what is politically correct, and what is fashionable. Search for truth, purpose, and meaning in everything you do. Look at what drives people and what the nature of the world is. Be comfortable with your thoughts, and put yourself out there; if someone asks, be willing to state your perspective. Strive to become a thought leader in business and have unique insights in private.

2. **Walk your own path.** The direction you set for yourself and the interests you pursue should be yours. Work to lead rather than to follow. Don't let others define where you head or how you act.

3. **Determine your values.** The independent person will have a strong focus on personal values. A constant refinement of these is important. Ethics in business and in private are essential. The world around us has its own value system. Yours should be very different. If you value what the world values, and let your definition of right and wrong be decided by the ever-changing political and social landscape, then you are not independent.

4. **Define your goals and dreams.** If you have the ability to capture and identify your goals and dreams, and can execute on them, you are walking a path few others will ever walk. While everyone has the capacity to do this, few ever take the time or know the steps required. You are truly independent and self-sufficient if you know what you want.

5. **Take risks.** Truly independent people are seen as risk takers, though the risk is usually relative. Being in business for yourself is often seen as risky, but the reality is that it is less risky than working for someone else. Risk taking, real and perceived, is the hallmark of the independent person. You can't achieve anything worthwhile if you don't take risks.

6. **Invest in yourself.** This does not mean buying yourself material possessions. Instead, it means taking the time to build yourself by investing time, money, and effort. If you are not constantly trying to better yourself, mentally and physically, you will either stagnate or fail. Independence is made up of constant self-improvement.

7. **Execute quickly on ideas.** When you know that a specific task needs to be done to make something happen, do it. When you decide to do something, do it today, not tomorrow. One primary difference between someone who is successful and truly independent from someone who never makes progress is that the independent person is able to move forward immediately with what needs to be done.

8. **Share your knowledge, wealth, and success.** The more you share what you have, the more that will come back to you. No one has ever gone bankrupt for giving generously. Your knowledge, wealth, and success were hard earned, but all of it came from elsewhere. Give generously of everything that you have gained, whether intellectual, material, or experiential.

Rule Not everyone can be helped, and not everyone will see your generosity as positive. Everyone is in a different place in life, and you can never tell where people are at in their own journey, or whether they are committed to changing. If you see a situation where you believe you can make a difference by giving, move forward if the recipient expresses sincere interest. Give what you are able, do so with energy and enthusiasm, and realize that the receiver may end up ungrateful or hostile toward you, as giving doesn't always result in the change either the giver or the receiver expected.

---

9. **Keep everyone's best interest in mind.** Independence does not mean shunning community or becoming an antisocial hermit. In all of your actions, try to determine what the best step to take is based on how it will impact others. Selfishness should not be an attribute of the independent person.

10. **Create.** You have the capacity to create something new, rather than simply riding the wave that others have made before you. You are not held back in what you can do. Finances are not an issue. Basic necessities are met. You have the responsibility and freedom to create and build a life that allows you to open up opportunities for others and alter the world around you based on your vision and idealism.

The Importance of the Interior Life

You likely have noticed an undercurrent in this book pertaining to the mystical aspect of business: if you put yourself out there, good things will happen. If you pursue advertising and marketing with the right intent, clients will find you. If you hire a mentor, you will learn new skills that will lead to new project work. If you invest a sizeable amount of money in your business, growth will occur. If you follow certain steps with the right intention, positive results will occur. Whether this is true because of the laws of the material world or the phenomena of the nonmaterial world, either way there are unseen forces at play that don't allow themselves to be easily defined by scientific formulas or modern society's conception of reality.

This is not a statement that a specific faith is required. It is a statement that if you want great things to happen in your life, and you want to succeed where others are not succeeding, then you must be able to acknowledge that there are greater forces at work in the world than can be seen. You must explore and work to grow in your understanding of the powers outside of yourself, both as they impact the business world and as they influence your everyday life.

In her foreword to *Woman Who Glows in the Dark*, (Tarcher, 2000) Clarissa Pinkola Estés writes

> *Pressure to conform for scant reward, and/or threats of marginalization because of one's beliefs, may force an individual to attempt to assimilate into this [material] layer of culture, thereby causing one's relationship to all things to slowly become defective. There, one becomes disconnected from the observable essence, from the affecting vitality of all things. It is not supposed to be this way for humans. Relationship to all matters and aspects of the world is meant to be complementary, wherein one is able to feel the electricity, and the condition of the electricity, inside of all things.*

This electricity is implicit in your life, and in your business. You can tap into some of the laws that surround these unseen forces and see how they impact your life, both professional and private. Understanding and acknowledging these forces and laws will have profound effects on everything that you see and interact with. If you want true success in both business and life, exploration and study of these forces and the interior life is critical. It is the secret ingredient that separates the moderately successful from those who truly live and work at their maximum potential. It is also the single most important factor in ensuring that your wealth and independence are built on a strong and sustainable foundation.

■ **Rule** Your spiritual life is a significant component of your physical well being and your ability to achieve those things in life that you seek to achieve. You cannot function at your greatest capacity if you have closed off your connection with the nonmaterial, or if your spiritual health is weak or sickly. All business is influenced by this, whether acknowledged or not.

Conclusion

It is time to take action. No matter where you currently are at in your professional path, you can take steps to advance on the path to wealth and independence. If you are a developer who has deep skills and is working for an employer, find a client who has contract work that you can do during off hours. If you are a technical consultant working for a large consulting firm, ask your management whether they would be interested in continuing to work with you if you were no longer an employee, but an independent contractor. If you are fresh out of college with an interest in a coding career, get yourself a job and some experience, and focus on your own education and discipline. If you are already an independent contractor and you've reached a basic level of success, push yourself to the next level and see if you can double your income and eliminate your travel. Use the concepts in this book, and experiment with your own techniques. Whatever you do, never stagnate, always keep moving, set high goals and dream big, seek freedom and change, take your business seriously, stay healthy, and realize that you have the ability to achieve great wealth and true independence if you want to.

Index

I

A

Advertising and marketing
  branding, 95–96
  collateral material, 93–95
  description, 82
  entrepreneurial people, 81
  publishing technical literature
    (see Publishing)
  solo practitioner, 82
  web presence, 92–93

B

Business investing
  abundance mentality, 177
  in charity, 187–188
  in clients, 185–186
  competition, 179–181
  economics, 177
  nonbusiness activities, 182
  in partners, 184–185
  in personal interests, 187
  risks, 182
  social environments, 178
  spending, 188–189
  subcontractors and employees, 183–184

Business structures
  business banking account, 69
  C-Corp, 67
  coder and service provider, 65
  creation, 67–69
  description, 63
  EIN, 69
  infrastructure, 77–79

insurance, 73–76
  LLC, 66
  partnership, 67
  payroll, 71–73
  protections, 64
  retirement planning, 79
  S-Corp, 66
  taxes, 69–71
  unincorporated sole
    roprietorship/DBA, 65

Business travel
  critical, 4–5
  essential rules
    (see Rules, business travel)
  long-distance and local client visits, 4
  mental motion, 11
  necessity, 2
  noncritical, 6
  redefining the rules, 6–7
  resting to mobile position, 2–3
  types, 4
  unnecessary travel, avoidance, 7–8

C

C-Corporation (C-Corp), 67

Certified Public Accountant (CPA), 71

Collateral material
  blogging, 95
  business cards, 94
  marketing materials, 94
  self-published print,
    electronic and audio books, 94
  social media, 95

Get the eBook for only $10!

> Now you can take the weightless companion with you anywhere, anytime. Your purchase of this book entitles you to 3 electronic versions for only $10.

This Apress title will prove so indispensible that you'll want to carry it with you everywhere, which is why we are offering the eBook in 3 formats for only $10 if you have already purchased the print book.

Convenient and fully searchable, the PDF version enables you to easily find and copy code—or perform examples by quickly toggling between instructions and applications. The MOBI format is ideal for your Kindle, while the ePUB can be utilized on a variety of mobile devices.

Go to www.apress.com/promo/tendollars to purchase your companion eBook.

All Apress eBooks are subject to copyright. All rights are reserved by the Publisher, whether the whole or part of the material is concerned, specifically the rights of translation, reprinting, reuse of illustrations, recitation, broadcasting, reproduction on microfilms or in any other physical way, and transmission or information storage and retrieval, electronic adaptation, computer software, or by similar or dissimilar methodology now known or hereafter developed. Exempted from this legal reservation are brief excerpts in connection with reviews or scholarly analysis or material supplied specifically for the purpose of being entered and executed on a computer system, for exclusive use by the purchaser of the work. Duplication of this publication or parts thereof is permitted only under the provisions of the Copyright Law of the Publisher's location, in its current version, and permission for use must always be obtained from Springer. Permissions for use may be obtained through RightsLink at the Copyright Clearance Center. Violations are liable to prosecution under the respective Copyright Law.

Other Apress Business Titles You Will Find Useful

Why Startups Fail
Feinleib
978-1-4302-4140-9

Startup
Ready
978-1-4302-4718-5

Success as a Programmer
Harper
978-1-4842-2005-5

Getting a Business Loan
Kiisel
978-1-4302-4998-1

The Street Smart MBA
Berghoff/Marovitz
978-1-4302-4700-6

Design Thinking for Entrepreneurs and Small Businesses
Ingle
978-1-4302-6181-6

Financial Modeling for Business Owners and Entrepreneurs
Sawyer
978-1-4842-0371-3

Know and Grow the Value of Your Business
McDaniel
978-1-4302-4786-0

Tax Strategies for the Small Business Owner
Fox
978-1-4302-4842-3

Available at www.apress.com

Other Apress Business Titles You Will Find Useful

Success in Programming
Harper
978-1-4842-0002-5

Startup
Ready
978-1-4302-4218-5

Why Startups Fail
Feinleib
978-1-4302-4140-9

Design Thinking for Entrepreneurs and Small Businesses
Ingle
978-1-4302-6181-0

The Street Smart MBA
Babitsky/Mangraviti
978-1-4302-4767-8

Getting a Business Loan
Kiisel
978-1-4302-4998-6

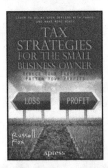

Tax Strategies for the Small Business Owner
Fox
978-1-4302-4842-2

Know and Grow the Value of Your Business
McDaniel
978-1-4302-4785-2

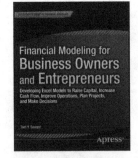

Financial Modeling for Business Owners and Entrepreneurs
Sawyer
978-1-4842-0371-2

Available at www.apress.com